END TIME SERIES

THE

RAPTURE

AND

THE

SECOND COMING

EXPLAINED

SAM AYOADE

C O N T E N T S

PREFACE

SECTION ONE
THE RAPTURE

CHAPTER

SECTION TWO
DISCOURSE – DIFFERENT RAPTURE VIEWS

SECTION THREE
TRIBULATION AND GREAT TRIBULATION

SECTION FOUR
THE SECOND COMING OF CHRIST

PREFACE

The Rapture of the Church is an integral part of the events of the end times. The growing interest in Bible prophecy has led to a plethora of literature and articles on the Rapture and the Second Coming of Christ. Yet, many Christians who are yearning for biblical truth are left confused about these related concepts simply because of divergence of opinion constantly put forward by theologians and Bible scholars. Although there is unanimity of opinion on the concept of Rapture, its timing has been a subject of intense controversy. This has left many questions unanswered:

Is the Rapture and the Second Coming of Christ one and the same event or separate events? In other words, Is the coming of Christ a single event or a two-phase event?
Is the Rapture before or after the Tribulation?
Will believers have to go through the Tribulation?

Sometimes, it is difficult to decide whether a Scripture is referring to the Rapture or to the Second Coming of Christ. The element of ambiguity surrounding these prophetic events has constituted a limiting factor to a clear understanding of end-time prophecy. Many have been needlessly caught up in the theological conflict between "pre-tribulation" and "post-tribulation" rapture views. This has resulted in a growing disenchantment among Christians and general apathy among a good majority of pastors, teachers and preachers who have become less motivated to teach and preach about these prophetic concepts. This has created a knowledge gap and conceptual vacuum that must be filled. To continue to ignore this need will be a great disservice to those who are thirsty for knowledge of the Word of God.

This book is designed to present the concept and various views of Rapture in a simple and concise manner. It also seeks to bring clarity to the atmosphere of ambiguity pervading the teaching, debate and understanding of the doctrine of Rapture and the Second Coming of Christ.

May the Lord illuminate our hearts with the truth of His Word that we may get ourselves ready for His appearing.

SECTION ONE

THE RAPTURE

BOOK CHAPTER 1

CONCEPT AND D E F I N I T I O N OF RAPTURE

Concept
The doctrine of Rapture is an offshoot of Eschatology. Eschatology is defined as the study of the last things or the biblical study of the future events. It is derived from the Greek word eschatos, which means "last."

Definition
The word "Rapture" is derived from the Latin word rapio or rapturo (seize or snatch) which is the translation of the Greek word harpazo (which means: "caught up", "to snatch or take away"). Although the word "Rapture" is not specifically found in the Bible, several passages allude to it.

In Christian eschatology, the Rapture refers to the belief that believers who have died shall be raised and believers who are alive shall be transformed and caught up together with them to meet the Lord in the air.

The relevant scripture passages include:
1 Thessalonians 4:16-17
"For the Lord Himself will descend from heaven with a shout, with the voice of an archangel and with the trumpet of God. And the dead in Christ will rise first. Then we who are alive and remain shall be caught

up together with them in the clouds to meet the Lord in the air. And thus we shall always be with the Lord."

1 Corinthians 15:51-53

"Behold, I tell you a mystery: We shall not all sleep, but we shall all be changed. In a moment, in the twinkling of an eye, at the last trumpet. For the trumpet will sound, and the dead will be raised incorruptible, and we shall be changed. For this corruptible must put on incorruption, and this mortal must put on immortality."

John 14:1-3

"Let not your heart be troubled; you believe in God, believe also in Me. In My Father's house are many mansions; if it were not so, I would have told you. I go to prepare a place for you. And if I go, I will come again and receive you to Myself; that where I am there you may be also.

BOOK CHAPTER 2

THE RAPTURE VERSUS THE SECOND COMING

The Rapture is an occasion when the bridegroom (Christ) comes for His bride (The Church) while His Second Coming is when He comes with His bride (the Church) to judge the world.

This brings to the fore the argument that the coming of the Lord will be in two stages. The opponents of this view argue that nowhere has the Bible clearly stated that His coming will be in two stages. However, the counter argument against this opposition is that a closer study of Scripture reveals two separate events pointing to two separate occasions of His coming.

The argument surrounding the Rapture is not so much about its reality but mainly about the timing. The following apparent distinctions between both events suggest different timings of occurrence.

DISTINCTIONS BETWEEN THE RAPTURE AND THE SECOND COMING

1. The Rapture will be secret (**1 Thessalonians 4:16-17**); while the Second Coming will be public
(**all eyes shall see Him – Revelation 1:7**).

2. At the Rapture, Jesus Christ will be met in the air (**1Thes. 4:17**), but in His Second Coming, He will come back to earth with His feet

touching upon the Mount of Olive – **Zechariah 14:4.**

3. The Rapture will occur when Jesus Christ comes for His bride (The Church); His Second Coming will occur when He comes with His bride to overthrow evil and judge the world.

4. The Rapture precedes the Tribulation while His Second Coming occurs at the end the Tribulation.

5. No signs precede the Rapture, while various signs would precede the Second Coming (**Matthew 24: 6-22**)

5. The Rapture focuses on the Redemption of the Church while the Second Coming focuses on the Redemption of Israel.

6. The arguments for and against the above key points will be discussed later in Section Two of this book.

BOOK CHAPTER 3

DIFFERENT VIEWS ON THE TIMING OF THE RAPTURE

The timing of the Rapture is one of the most controversial concepts in biblical eschatology.

Most Bible scholars agree on the concept of Rapture but differ on the timing. The three major views on the timing of the Rapture are:

1. PRETRIBULATION RAPTURE

This view advocates that the Rapture will occur before the seven-year tribulation period while the Second Coming will occur at the end of the tribulation period.

The main Scriptural evidence for this view is:

1 Thessalonians 4:15-17 KJV
"For this we say unto you by the word of the Lord, that we which are alive and remain unto the coming of the Lord shall not precede them which are asleep. For the Lord Himself shall descend from heaven with a shout, with the voice of the archangel, and with the trump of God; and the dead in Christ shall rise first. Then we which are alive and remain shall be caught up together with them in the clouds, to meet the Lord in the air; and so shall we ever be with the Lord."

Pre-tribulationists believe that true Christians, along with resurrected saints, will be taken up physically (raptured) before the tribulation begins. So far, the Holy Spirit has been restraining the man of lawlessness (The antichrist) but when the Church is raptured the Holy Spirit (which is the restraining force) will be removed, then making way for the antichrist and the tribulation. The Holy Spirit will not operate on earth during the Tribulation Period. This idea is supported by:

2 Thessalonians 2:6-7.

"And Now you know what is restraining, that he may be revealed in his own time. For the mystery of lawlessness is already at work; only He who now restraints will do so until He is taken out of the way."

After the Tribulation, Christ will return to earth with His saints. His Second Coming (and not the Rapture) will occur after the tribulation as confirmed by the following passage, among others:

"Immediately after the tribulation of those days shall the sun be darkened, and the moon shall not give her light, and the stars shall fall from heaven, and the powers of the heavens shall be shaken. And then shall appear the sign of the Son of man in heavens: and then shall all the tribes of the earth mourn, and they shall see the Son of man coming in the clouds of heaven with power and great glory. And He shall send His angels with a great sound of trumpet, and they shall gather together his elect from the four winds, from one end of heaven to the other" – **Matthew 24:29-31 KJV.**

Pre-tribulationists believe that the "elect" mentioned here are the tribulation saints while post-tribulationists believe they include the Church saints. In actual fact, Church saints will be in heaven with Christ prior to the Tribulation period and they will accompany Him on His Second Coming.

"And the armies in heaven, clothed in fine linen, white and clean, followed Him on white horses" – **Revelation 19:14.**

Notice the plural form of "armies" which denotes angelic army and the army of saints that had been raptured.

2. MIDTRIBULATION RAPTURE

This view holds that the Rapture will occur half-way through the Tribulation Period, that is, at the end of the first half (three and half years) of the seven-year period. Midtribulationists believe that the Church will be removed just before the latter half – three-and-a-half year-period - which will be dominated by the outpouring of the wrath of God on those who reject Him. The main passage quoted in support of this view is:

"For God has not destined us for wrath, but to obtain salvation through our Lord Jesus Christ" – **1 Thessalonians 5:9.**

3. POSTRIBULATION RAPTURE

Post-tribulation rapture view holds that the Rapture will occur at the end of the seven-year tribulation period and that Christians will remain on earth throughout the seven-year Tribulation Period. This is a complete contrast to the pre-tribulation rapture view.

Evidence for this view includes the first resurrection, mentioned in Revelation 20:5, which is the resurrection of tribulation martyrs after the Second Coming of Christ as mentioned in verse 4. Hence post-tribulationists believe that since this first resurrection occurs after the Tribulation, it follows that Rapture can only be post-tribulational.

The main biblical evidence relied upon by this view is captured in the following passage:

"But the rest of the dead did not live again until the thousand years were finished. This is the first resurrection. Blessed and holy is he who has part in the first resurrection. Over such the second death has no power, but they shall be priests of God and of Christ, and shall reign with Him a thousand years" – **Revelation 20:5-6.**

In essence, post-tribulationists consider the Rapture and the Second Coming of Christ as a single event.

BOOK CHAPTER 4

TRIBULATION IN RELATION TO THE RAPTURE OF THE CHURCH

We have considered the different viewpoints on the timing of the Rapture. One central question is whether Christ's return will occur as a single event or two separate events.

The first event is the Rapture when true Christians who are alive, along with resurrected believers, will be caught up in the cloud to meet Jesus in the air. This "catching up" will occur before the seven-year Tribulation period also known as the 70th week of Daniel. During this event, Christ will not come to earth, He will be in the air to receive His own. This is a secret appearance only to be witnessed by the Church saints.

The second event is the Second Coming of Christ which occurs at the end of the seven-year Tribulation. This is a public appearance to be witnessed by all eyes. On this occasion, Christ will come back to earth with His saints who had been raptured prior to the Tribulation.

Post-tribulation View

On the other hand, the post-tribulation rapture view holds that both the Rapture and the Second Coming will be a single event. The proponents argue that after the Tribulation the saints will be raptured to meet Christ in the air and then immediately come back to earth with Him. This view negates Christ's promise in **John 14:3** "And if I go and prepare a place for you, I will come again and receive you unto myself; that where I am there you may be also." The weakness of post-tribulation rapture view is obvious and its premise is without biblical foundation.

Mid-tribulation View
Midtribulationalism holds that the Rapture will occur at the mid-point of the Tribulation, that is, after the first three and a half years.

Pre-tribulation View
The credible view is that the Rapture will occur before the Tribulation period. To support this concept, we need to recognise the fact that these two events – Rapture and Tribulation - have two different purposes.
The purpose of Tribulation is to unleash God's punishment upon the world The purpose of Rapture is to save the Church from the wrath of God.

Despite several scriptural supports for this concept, advocates of posttribulationalism find it hard to accept the above programme of divine judgment and salvation. Their main argument is that the Scripture does not indicate anywhere that the Rapture will precede the Tribulation period. The simple answer to that is that nowhere does the Scripture indicate that the Rapture will occur after the Tribulation period.

The post-tribulational view encourages Christians to be complacent. Believing that the Rapture is not imminent but far away beyond the tribulation period and after the signs preceding His second coming, can only result in lack of preparedness by treating the concept of Rapture with levity and as a matter devoid of urgency. Just like the servant in **Matthew 24:48-49**, thinking his master would delay His coming, started maltreating his fellow servants but only to be caught unawares by his Master's unannounced arrival.

It is not only biblical but indeed safe to hold the view that the Rapture will occur before the Tribulation. To believe otherwise is unwise and risky. We should behave like the wise virgins in the Bible where Jesus warns us to be spiritually prepared – **Matthew 25:1-10.** We must be in a state of constant preparedness because:

1. Rapture is imminent. Unlike the second coming It will occur instantaneously without warning and without preceding signs. We must be spiritually alert, eagerly awaiting His imminent appearance. I can't wait to see Jesus. What about you?

2. Rapture is too great an opportunity to be missed. To be forewarned is to be forearmed.

3. The posture of waiting, watching, readiness and alertness is the will of Christ for His Church as commanded in the Scripture.

Luke 12:40
"You also must be ready for the Son of Man is coming at an hour you do not expect."

2 Peter 3:10
"But the day of the Lord will come like a thief…"

Mark 13:37
"And what I say to you, I say to all: Watch!."

BOOK CHAPTER 5

THE WAY FORWARD
(The concept of Rapture should not be relegated to the background)

The unfolding course of events around the world today is a constant reminder that we are inching closer and closer to the fulfilment of Bible prophecy of the end times. This is not to say that the prophecies are being completely fulfilled now but we are moving closer to the first phase of the signs – wars, rumours of wars, natural disasters, plague, political unrest etc. – preceding the Second Coming of Christ. For centuries, decades and years, believers have been waiting in anticipation but yet no one knows when the Lord will come. For this reason, we should shift our position from a state of discouragement to a state of readiness.

"Therefore, you also be ready, for the Son of Man is coming at an hour you do not expect." **Matthew 24:44**

In his epistle to the Colossians, Paul admonishes believers to "seek those things which are above, where Christ is, sitting at the right hand of God" (**Colossians 3:1**). He also advises them to set their minds on things above, not on things on the earth. These words are equally applicable to us especially now that we see the day approaching. Paul's central message is encapsulated in verse 4 of the third chapter of his epistle to the Colossians:

"When Christ who is our life appears, then you also will appear with Him in glory" – **Colossians 3:4**

This describes the ultimate stage of our spiritual life when we will be glorified with Christ in heaven. Now is the time to focus our attention beyond our present state, and our affection beyond the realm of this present age, beyond the corruption of this perverted world. As children of God, redeemed through the precious blood of Jesus Christ, we should remain in earnest expectation of His appearance, constantly reminded by the fact that knowing Him now is the beginning of our journey to glory.

"Beloved, now we are children of God, and it has not yet been revealed what we shall be, but we know that when He is revealed, we shall be like Him, for we shall see Him as He is" – **1 John 3:2.**

It is reassuring to know that Christ our King will soon be revealed in majesty and splendor and we will join him in the glory of His majesty dressed in the immaculate garment of purity and robe of righteousness, immortality and incorruption. We all shall forever be together with Him.

Over the years, I have discovered that, among Christians, the biggest factor responsible for the loss of interest in the doctrine of Rapture and the Second Coming of Christ is the myriads of opposing views on either side of the arguments concerning the timing of the Rapture. The lack of unanimity and the divergence of opinion should in no way deter believers from taking this important doctrine seriously. Teachers and preachers of the Word should fast track the teaching of the Rapture and the Second Coming of Christ to the top of their priority list and to the forefront of their programme. This will help free the mind of an average Christian from being preoccupied with the cares of this world. It is time to heed the call to be ready because the Son of Man will come at an hour we do not expect.

The recurring bone of contention has always been whether the Rapture will occur before the Tribulation or after. The divided opinion has led to the tendency of one group claiming superiority of opinion over the other with a view to scoring unnecessary theological point. For us, now is the time to strive hard to overcome this tendency with a view to restoring the much-needed interest of the vast majority of Christians in the doctrine of the end times especially in the face of the available overwhelming scriptural evidence. Can we afford to be so embroiled in this theological conflict to the detriment of our watchfulness? Neither the author nor the reader of this book wants to run the risk of being caught unawares. Is it not better to be safe than be sorry? Why should we continue to be dispassionate about the coming of the Lord? The doctrine of Rapture should be brought to the fore rather than being relegated to the background in our study of the Word of God. Then what is the way forward?

The way forward is to continually look forward to the manifestation of our glorious union with the Lord. The coming of the Lord is a blessed hope and a hope above all hopes. The prospect of His unexpected arrival puts us on our guard.

The way forward is to always put our spiritual lives in order. We cannot afford to be complacent or half-hearted about our Christian living.

The way forward is to constantly remember our unique position in this world that though we are in the world, we are not of the world because our citizenship is in heaven.

The way forward is to keep our eyes on Jesus while we run our race with unwavering expectation of His return.

The way forward is to be filled with joy knowing that our present redemption will soon be translated to our future destiny with Christ.

As we navigate the uncertain seasons of the end times, let us forget what is behind and focus on what is ahead of us and reach out for the things ahead. We should constantly pursue righteousness and holiness and keep away from those things in our lives that are keeping us away from being completely devoted to Christ and His will. This is echoed by Paul in **Philippians 3:13-14.** Further down in verse 20, he reminds us that **"our citizenship is in heaven from which we eagerly wait for the Saviour, the Lord Jesus Christ."** The way forward is to always look forward to heaven and the coming of our Lord Jesus Christ.

Let us watch therefore, for we know neither the day nor the hour in which the Son of Man is coming.

SECTION TWO
DISCOURSE - DIFFERENT RAPTURE VIEWS

BOOK CHAPTER 6

CONFUSION AND ARGUMENTS ABOUT THE TIMING OF THE RAPTURE

The concept of Rapture is one of the most contested element of end-time theological scholarship. Although there is general unanimity of views about the concept, the timing of it has been the subject of sharp disagreement among Bible scholars. As earlier discussed, the Rapture is the doctrine that at the appearance of Christ in the air, believers who are alive will be caught up to meet Him following the resurrection and catching up of believers who were dead.

Teachings concerning the Rapture were not widely disseminated until the nineteenth century. Since then, three distinct views have emerged. The major views are:
Pre-tribulation Rapture
Mid-tribulation Rapture
Post-tribulation Rapture

Before examining these major views, it is pertinent to highlight two main considerations relevant to the concept of Rapture.

THE EXTENT OF RAPTURE
One of the questions often asked is whether there is going to be a total

rapture or a partial rapture. In other words, are all believers or only certain believers going to be raptured?

1. Partial Rapture

Partial Rapture teaches that only true and faithful believers who are watching and waiting for the Lord will be raptured while the unfaithful Christians will be left behind to go through the pain and agony of the wrath of God in the seven-year Tribulation period. This theory is predicated on the New Testament passages that emphasise on obedience. For instance, in Matthew 7:21, Jesus states that "Not everyone who calls me Lord, Lord, will enter the Kingdom of heaven but he who does the will of My Father in heaven."

2. Rapture of All Believers

However, some find it hard to believe the partial rapture theory because of the Bible passage in 1 Corinthians 15:51 which states:

We shall not all sleep, but we shall all be changed.

Some also believe that 1 Thessalonians 4:13-18 refers to all believers. Others have also misinterpreted the story of the ten virgins in Matthew 25:1-13, saying that the five unwise virgins refer to unbelievers. This is a wrong interpretation because unbelievers will not be watching and waiting for the groom (Jesus Christ). All ten virgins represent all believers – some are ready, some are not.

Conclusion

It would be conceptually reckless to believe that all believers would be raptured irrespective of how they live their lives. This view seems to overlook the need for a Christian to live a life of obedience to God. It encourages living a reckless life. It is an undeniable fact that many professing Christians still live in their sinful and canal past. Some have backslidden; many pretend to serve God while secretly following other gods. Many do serve God and mammon at the same time. Sanctification means nothing to many. Some are engaged in drunkenness, envy and other acts of unrighteousness. They have ignored the warnings in the Scripture that "those who practise such things" will not enter the Kingdom of God:

Galatian 5:21
"… …Just as I also told you in time past, that those who practice such things will not inherit the kingdom of God.

1 Corinthians 6:9-10
"Do you not know that the unrighteous will not inherit the kingdom of God? Do not be deceived. Neither fornicators, nor idolaters, nor adulterers, nor homosexuals, nor sodomites, nor thieves nor covetous, nor drunkards, nor revilers, nor extortioners will inherit the kingdom of God."

The doctrine of eternal security is sometimes referred to as "once saved, always saved." In other words, once you get saved, you cannot be disinherited of the kingdom of God regardless of what you do. What happened to Judas Iscariot then? People are being deceived by this erroneous belief. They are taking the grace of God for granted by trying to trap people in this dangerous delusion.

We must remember that as sinners we were not saved to remain sinners but saved to become saints. A worthy servant must remain obedient to his Master. Hence Paul often refers to himself as a "bondservant of Jesus Christ." A servant is no longer subject to his own will but to the will of the Master.

THE TIMING OF RAPTURE
Essentially, there are three major views about the timing of the Rapture which will be discussed in the subsequent chapters. These are:

Pretibulationalism (Pre-trib)
Midtribulationalism (Mid-trib)
Posttribulationalism (Post-trib)

BOOK CHAPTER 7

PRE-TRIBULATION RAPTURE VIEW-POINTS

PRETIBULATIONALISM

This view teaches that the Rapture will occur before the beginning of the seven-year Tribulation Period. This view considers that God's dispensation for the Church is distinct from His dispensation for Israel. The Tribulation period is part of God's programme for Israel after the rapture of the Church.

There are several scriptural bases in favour of this view. Let us examine some of the biblical evidence in support.

i. IMMINENCE

This doctrine teaches that Jesus could come any time. Therefore, rapture could happen without any warning or predicted events. All the end-time signs enumerated in the Scripture relate to the Second Coming of Christ. Imminence can be gleaned from many Bible passages. Bible passages relating to the Rapture clearly teaches imminence while those relating to the Second Coming do not. Passages that teach imminence include:

1 Thessalonians 5:4

"But you, brethren, are not in darkness, so that the Day should overtake you as a thief."

Matthew 24:42-43

"Watch therefore, for you do not know what hour your Lord is coming.

But know this, that if the master of the house had known what hour the thief would come, he would have watched and not allowed his house to be broken into."

Mark 13:32-33
"But of that day or that hour no one knows, not even the angels in heaven, nor the Son, but only the Father. Take heed, watch; for you do not know when the time will come."

Mark 13:35-37
"Watch therefore, for you do not know when the master of the house is coming – in the evening, at mid-night, at the crowing of the rooster, or in the morning, lest, coming suddenly, he finds you sleeping."

Luke 12:40
"You also must be ready; for the Son of man is coming at an unexpected hour."

James 5:7-8
"Therefore, be patient, brethren, until the coming of the Lord. See how the farmer waits for the precious fruit of the earth, waiting patiently for it until it receives the early and latter rain. You also be patient. Establish your hearts, for the coming of the Lord is at hand."

Titus 2:12-13
"Teaching us that, denying ungodliness and worldly lusts, we should live soberly, righteously, and godly in the present age. Looking for the blessed hope and glorious appearing of our great God and Saviour, Jesus Christ."

Note:
These passages are devoid of preceding signs but convey the message about suddenness and the need to live a godly life in anticipation of the coming of the Lord.

ii. THE DAY OF THE LORD

The Day of the Lord has been misconceived by many to mean the Rapture. These are two different events. The Day of the Lord is the time of ultimate outpouring of God's wrath upon the world which is encapsulated in the events of the Tribulation Period. The Rapture occurs before the Day of the Lord. Below are some of the prophecies concerning the Day of the Lord:

Zephaniah 1:14-17
"The great day of the Lord is near; It is near and hastens quickly. The noice of the day of the Lord is bitter; There the mighty men shall cry out. That day is a day of wrath. A day of trouble and distress; A day of devastation and desolation; A day of darkness and gloominess; A day of clouds and thick darkness. I will bring distress upon men, and they shall walk like blind men, because they have sinned against the Lord. Their blood shall be poured out like dust, and their flesh like refuse."

Joel 1:15
"Alas for the day! For the day of the Lord is at hand.

Amos 5:18
"Woe to you who desire the day of the Lord! For what good is the day of the Lord to you? It will be darkness and not light."

Isaiah 13:9-11
"Behold, the day of the Lord comes, Cruel, with both wrath and fierce anger, to lay the land desolate. And He will destroy its sinners from it. For the stars of heaven and their constellations will not give their light; The sun will be darkened in its going forth, and the moon will not cause its light to shine. I will punish the world for its evil."

Jeremiah 46:10
"For this is the day of the Lord God of hosts. A day of vengeance, that He may avenge Himself on His adversaries. The sword shall devour; it shall be satiated and made drunk with their blood."

The Church will be saved from the coming Wrath.

The Church will not experience the Day of the Lord in the sense that the Rapture would have occurred before the Tribulation Period. This view is further strengthened by the following biblical facts:

Revelation 3:10

"Because you have kept My command to persevere, I also will keep you from the hour of trial which shall come upon the whole world, to test those who dwell on the earth."

God has promised to keep the Church (the true believers who keep His Word) from the hour of trial which shall befall the whole world. God did not promise to protect the Church through the Tribulation as posttribulationists believe. If the effect of the Tribulation will be worldwide, affecting everyone on earth, how can the Church be on earth and still escape the wrath? When someone is kept from a horrible situation, it means that person has not experienced the horror of that situation. God's promise is:

"I will keep you from the hour of testing and
NOT
"I will protect you in the hour of testing.

It is clear from the foregoing that the Church will not experience the Tribulation as the posttribulationists would have us believe.

ABSENCE OF THE CHURCH DURING THE TRIBULATION PERIOD

One striking and undisputable fact supporting the absence of the Church during the tribulation period is that there is no mention of the Church anywhere between Revelation Chapter 5 and Chapter 19

SUMMARY

1. There is a clear distinction between the Rapture and the Second Coming of Christ because the Rapture will occur without warning while there are several signs preceding the Second Coming.

2. There are several scriptural passages confirming the imminence of Rapture and supporting the two-phase return of Christ. These passages should be subject to literal interpretation rather than applying allegorical interpretation in order to sustain the postribulational views.

3. God has promised to keep the Church from the hour of trial to come

4. There is no mention of the Church throughout the tribulation events between **Revelation 5 and Revelation 19.**

BOOK CHAPTER 8

MID-TRIBULATION RAPTURE VIEW-POINTS

B. MIDTRIBULATIONALISM

This view teaches that the Rapture will occur at the mid-point of the seven-year Tribulation period, in other words, immediately after the first three and half years of the Tribulation Period. The Church will be on earth during the first three and a half years but will be raptured immediately before the commencement of the Great Tribulation.

Proponents of this view believe that the latter half of the tribulation period, being the Great Tribulation, will be the time when the intense judgment of God will be poured upon the earth This time, they believe, will be immediately preceded by the Rapture of the Church. They are of the view that the Church will go through the first three-and-a-half-year period of tribulation. Scriptural support for this view includes the following passages:

2 Thessalonians 2:3
"Let no one deceive you by any means, that day will not come unless the falling away comes first and the man of sin is revealed from heaven, the son of perdition."

Daniel 9:27
"Then he shall confirm a covenant with many for one week (seven years); but in the middle of the week, he shall bring an end to sacrifice and offering, and on the wing of abominations shall be one who makes desolate … …"

Daniel 7:25

"He shall speak pompous words against the Most High; shall persecute the saints of the Most High, and shall intend to change times and law. Then the saints shall be given into his hand for a time and times and half a time.

These passages refer to the time when the antichrist will break his covenant with Israel which is expected to happen about the mid-point of the Tribulation Period.

Another foundational belief of the mid-tributationists is that the trumpet of **1 Corinthians 15:52** is the same as the one in **Revelation11:15.**

Let us compare both passages:

1 CORINTHIANS 15:52	REVELATION 11:15
"In a moment, in the twinkling of an eye, at the last trumpet. For the trumpet will sound, and the dead will be raised incorruptible, and we shall be changed.	"Then the seventh angel sounded: And there were loud voices in heaven, saying, "The kingdoms of this world have become the kingdoms of our Lord and of His Christ, and He shall reign forever and ever!"

Whereas the trumpet in 1 Corinthians 15:52 is the trumpet that sounds at the rapture, the trumpet mentioned in Revelation 11:15 is the seventh judgment trumpet introducing the third woe comprising of the seven bowls of God's wrath to be poured on the earth.

These two trumpets have different objectives. It is illogical and erroneous to consider them to be the same. The mid-tribulationists are wrong in this regard.

Interpretation of "Wrath" in 1 Thessalonians 5:9

Although this passage indicates that the Church has not been appointed to suffer wrath but to receive salvation, midtribulationalism interprets "wrath" as only referring to the second half of the tribulation, ignoring the fact that all troubles poured out in the first half of tribulation are equally considered to be the wrath of God.

By and large, all the arguments advanced by mid-tribulationalism are not convincing.

BOOK CHAPTER 9

POST-TRIBULATION RAPTURE VIEW-POINTS

C. POSTTRIBULATIONALISM

Posttribulationalism teaches that:

(i)The Rapture occurs at the end of the Tribulation and that there is only one phase of the Second Coming of Christ, outrightly discounting the pretribulational two-phase view.

(ii)At the end of the Great Tribulation the Church will be caught up to meet Christ in the air and then return immediately to earth with Him for the commencement of His millennial reign.

(iii)That the Church will not be spared from the Tribulation.
Essentially, post-tribulationalism believes that the Church will go through the Tribulation period, claiming that nowhere does the Bible teach that the Rapture will occur before the Tribulation.

The counter argument is that nowhere does the Bible teach that the Rapture will occur after the Tribulation.

This unsustainable argument is based on **Matthew 24:21,30** which read:

"(21)For then there will be great tribulation, such as has not been since the beginning of the world until this time, no, nor ever shall be."

(29) "Immediately after the tribulation of those days, the sun will be

darkened, and the moon will not give its light; the stars will fall from heaven, and the powers of the heavens will be shaken."

(30) "Then the sign of the Son of Man will appear in heaven and then all the tribes of the earth will mourn, and they will see the Son of Man coming on the clouds of heaven with power and great glory.

COMMENTS.
These arguments are weak in many respects.
- Firstly, the above passages refer to the single event of the Second Coming of Christ and not to the Rapture.

- Secondly, the catching up of the Church is not mentioned here.

- Thirdly, it is inconceivable that the Church will be caught up to meet Christ in the air and then immediately do a U-turn back to earth. How does this correspond to Christ's promise that "I will come back to take you to Myself so that where I am you may be also"?

By and large, the posttribulational arguments listed above are, in every sense, untenable.

COMPARATIVE MERITS OF PRE-TRIBULATION RAPTURE VIEWS

The crux of the matter is the fact that the Rapture is distinct from the Second Coming of Christ. This view is clearly supported by the pre-tribulation rapture view with indisputable merits outlined below and amplified in the Epilogue section in Chapter 20 of this book:

1. Jesus Christ indirectly refers to pre-tribulation rapture in John 14:1-3 where He promises to come and take us to heaven so that where He is we may also be.

2. Pre-tribulation rapture view follows the literal interpretation of the Bible, strictly maintaining a consistent hermeneutical approach.
3. Pre-tribulationism recognises the distinction between Israel and the Church. The Church is taken to heaven at the Rapture while Israel will be saved after the Rapture during the Tribulation period. Hence the Church is not mentioned between **Revelation 5 and Revelation 19.**
4. Only the pre-tribulation rapture view emphasizes on the imminent nature of the Rapture. No signs precede the Rapture while many signs will precede the Second Coming of Christ.
5. Whereas the Second Coming of Christ was revealed to Old Testament prophets, Rapture is a mystery hidden from ages but revealed in the New Testament.
6. The Church is not appointed to wrath and will not experience the Tribulation – **Romans 5:9; 1 Thessalonians 5:9.**
7. Pre-tribulation rapture view recognises the 70th Week of Daniel as synonymous with the Tribulation period and as a period during which God's programme with Israel will be accomplished.
8. The Church must be raptured to heaven first for the Marriage of the lamb with the Church to take place. The bride (the Church) will come back with Christ to earth after the marriage and the Marriage Super in heaven.
9. Only the pre-tribulation rapture view draws a clear distinction, and rightly so, between the Rapture and the Second Coming. These are two separate events occurring on either side of the Tribulation Period – the Rapture before, and the Second Coming after.
10. The Restrainer (The Holy Spirit in-dwelling the Church) must be removed first in order to reveal the lawless one – the Antichrist – who dominates the Tribulation Period. **2 Thessalonians 2:7-8.**

BOOK CHAPTER 10.

THE OLIVET DISCOURSE
(MATTHEW CHAPTERS 24 AND 25)

The Olivet Discourse refers to the prophetic teaching of Jesus Christ on the Mount of Olives as recorded extensively in Matthew chapters 24 and 25 with parallel passages in Mark 13 and Luke 21. This discourse primarily details the signs preceding His Second Coming which will occur immediately after the seven-year Tribulation Period declared by Jesus in **Matthew 24:29-30:.**

"Immediately after the tribulation of those days the sun will be darkened, and the moon will not give its light; the stars will fall from heaven and the powers of the heaven will be shaken. Then the sign of the Son of Man will appear in heaven, and then all the tribes of the earth will mourn, and they will see the Son of Man coming on the clouds of heaven with power and great glory."

The Tribulation period is a time of great outpouring of God's wrath upon the unrepentant inhabitants of this world. Events unfolding around the world are undoubtedly indicative of the signs of the end times as revealed in the Scripture.

MATTHEW CHAPTER 24 - GENERAL GLOBAL SIGNS
In His Olivet Discourse on End-Times, Jesus gave some general signs that would signal the imminence of His Second Coming. The core of

this discourse is recorded in Matthew 24 with comparable passages in Mark 13 and Luke 21.

> **Matthew 24:1-2**
> **"Then Jesus went out and departed from the temple, and His disciples came up to show Him the buildings of the temple. And Jesus said to them: 'Do you not see all these things? Assuredly, I say to you, not one stone shall be left here upon another, that shall not be thrown down.' "**

Structural Grandeur

Jesus went out and departed from the temple as one who did not mean to return to the earthly temple, and then his disciples came to show Him the magnificent structure and the external ambience of the temple. Jesus immediately issued a prophetic response that none of the stones shall be left upon another that shall not be thrown down. This prophecy was literally fulfilled in AD 70 when the Roman army, led by Titus, completely destroyed the temple.

After the destruction of the First Temple (**Solomon's Temple**) by Nebuchadnezzar in 586 BC, this Second Temple was built by Zerubbabel and Ezra in 516 BC (**Ezra 6:15**) and later lavishly expanded and refurbished by Herod the Great who ruled when Jesus was born. The temple was so central to Jewish religious life and so sacred that speaking against it could be considered a blasphemy (**Acts 6:13**). Yet, Jesus unequivocally pronounced the impending destruction of the temple and the complete annihilation of its splendour.

Hence the interrogatory nature of Jesus' statement in verse 2: **"Do you not see all these things?"** Two lessons can be drawn from this:

- We can see how little God values magnificent houses of prayer when they are made to operate as dens of thieves and extortioners.

- The Most High does not dwell in temples made with hands – **Acts 7:48.** Do you not know that you yourselves are the temple of God and that the Spirit of God dwells in you? – 1 Corinthians 3:16

Matthew 24:3
Now as He sat on the Mount of Olives, the disciples came to Him privately, saying, "Tell us, when will these things be? And what will be the sign of Your coming and of the end of the age?"

It is noteworthy that the disciples asked Jesus two questions (some would say three, because the second question has a dual undertone).

1. When will these things happen?
2. What will be the sign of your coming and of the end of the world?

When will these things happen?
The disciples, having been pondering over Jesus' dismissive response to their introduction of the structural beauty of the temple hoping to get a flattering response, curiously asked to know when the events leading to the destruction of the temple would happen.

However, Jesus ignored the first question and went straight to addressing the second one regarding the sign of His Second Coming and the events of the end of the age. In answering this question, Jesus prophesied about the events that must occur between His Ascension and the time immediately before His Second Coming. Jesus describes what must be expected as follows:

1.   IMPOSTORS – Verses 4-5
And Jesus answered and said to them: " Take heed that no one deceives you. For many will come in My name, saying 'I am the Christ,' and will deceive many."

2.   WARS AND RUMOURS OF WAR – Verse 6
"And you will hear of wars and rumours of wars. See that you are not

troubled; for all these things must come to pass, but the end is not yet."

3. INTERNATIONAL UNREST AND NATURAL DISASTERS – Verses 7-8

"For nation will rise against nation, and kingdom against kingdom, and there will be famines, pestilences and earthquakes in various places. All these things are the beginning of sorrows"

4. PERSECUTION AND BETRAYAL – Verses 9-10

"Then they will deliver you up to tribulation and kill you, and you will be hated by all nations for My name's sake. And then many will be offended, will betray one another and will hate one another."

5. FALSE PROPHETS AND LAWLESSNESS– Verse s 11-12, 24

"Then many false prophets will rise up and deceive many. And because lawlessness will abound, the love of many will grow cold. "

6. GLOBAL SPREAD OF THE GOSPEL – Verse 14

"And this gospel of the kingdom will be preached in all the world as a witness to all the nations, and then the end will come."

7. THE ABOMINATION OF DESOLATION – Verses 15-20

"Therefore when you see the 'abomination of desolation' spoken of by Daniel the prophet, standing in the holy place, then let those who are in Judea flee to the mountain … … … ….."

8. GREAT TRIBULATION – Verses 21-28

"For then there will be great tribulation, such as has not been since the beginning of the world until this time no, nor ever shall be … … ….."

9. COMPLETE LUNAR AND SOLAR ECLIPSE – Verse 29

"Immediately after the tribulation of those days, the sun will be darkened,   and the moon will not give its light, the stars will fall from heaven, and the   powers of the heavens will be shaken."

10.   THE COMING OF CHRIST – Verse 30-31

"Then the sign of the Son of Man will appear in heaven, and then all the tribes of the earth will mourn, and they will see the Son of Man coming on the clouds of heaven with power and great glory. And He will send His angels with a great sound of a trumpet, and they will gather together His elect from the four winds, from one end of heaven to the other."

TO WHAT EXTENT HAVE THE ABOVE SIGNS BEEN FULFILLED?

It is not unreasonable to conclude that the first six of the above signs have been largely fulfilled.

(i) Impostors and false prophets have paraded themselves as ministers of the gospel in many countries, deceiving the unsuspecting believers and non-believers alike – all for material gains. The act of merchandising the gospel and monetizing prayer and prophecy seems to become the norm in modern day Church. The preaching of the gospel of repentance and salvation has been replaced with the gospel of prosperity and damnable heresies. In some Churches, God's favour and mercy are advertised in exchange for money. In other words, the amount of money you pay will determine the amount of favour and blessing you receive from God.

(ii) In the last few decades, wars have frequently broken out among nations with international conflicts pervading the political landscape. With the incessant escalation of tension, the world peace has become more fragile than ever before.

(iii) Plagues, flood, earthquake and severe fire outbreaks, have been experienced in many parts of the world.

(iv) On the other end of the spectrum, early Christians as well as contemporary believers have suffered betrayal, persecution and martyrdom on account of the gospel. Many countries are still hostile towards Christianity and the preaching of the gospel in such countries comes with great risks.

(v) False prophets are on the rise and have invaded the global cyber space.

(vi) Undoubtedly, the gospel has been preached to most part of the world except a few remote tribes who probably have not been reached.

IS ANY PART OF MATTHEW 24 RELEVANT TO THE RAPTURE?

A question that often comes to mind is whether the passages in Matthew 24 have application both to the Rapture and the Second Coming of Christ. A careful study of the whole chapter shows that the Rapture is referred to in the latter part of the Olivet Discourse.

MATTHEW 24:4-31

This passage narrates the events preceding the Second Coming of Christ. These events end with the seven-year Tribulation/Great Tribulation period, immediately after which Christ will come with power and great glory and send His angels to gather together His elect from one end of the heaven to the other.

A BRIDGE
Parable of the Fig Tree

Verses 32-35 form a bridge between the Second Coming discourse and the Rapture discourse. Jesus has been speaking about the signs and events leading up to His Second Coming, the timing of which will be clearly understood in the same way we can tell when a fig tree is about to produce fruits.

"Now learn this parable from the fig tree. When its branch has already become tender and puts forth leaves, you know that summer is near. So, you also when you see all these things, know that it is near – at the doors. Assuredly I say to you, this generation will by no means pass away till all these things take place. Heaven and earth will pass away, but My words will by no means pass away."

"This generation" referred to by Christ simply means the future generation, following the re-birth of Israel, will not end until all the events mentioned in the Olivet Discourse were fulfilled. This is the generation that will be in existence during those events and not the generation of his disciples. Another point to note is that these events constitute a sense of anticipation of His Second Coming seven years after the start of Tribulation. Hence Jesus was referring to the future generation that will endure the Tribulation as the generation that will not pass away while all these things happen.

CHANGE OF CONTEXT
Verse 36-46
A meticulous study of these verses reveals that the context of the Olivet discourse changes as Jesus begins describing a different set of events. In verse 35, Jesus had just finished describing His Second Coming (which can be known with some degree of precision) seven years after the start of the Tribulation.

However, in verse 36 Jesus says that there will be another day that is not knowable. Hence He begins this next section with the phrase "But of that day", speaking of a different day entirely. This comment introduces a new topic – the Rapture

The crux of His message from here on is **"Watch" and "Be ready"**. No more signs, nor preceding events. The Rapture will happen unexpectedly and without warning as the word itself was derived from the Latin word "Rapturo" or Greek word "Harpazo" which means "caught up." The imminent nature of Rapture requires there to be neither warnings nor signs.   Let us examine the following key points:

1. SECRET – VERSE 36
"But of that day and hour no one knows, not even the angels of heaven, but My Father only."

Note
Jesus could not possibly be referring to His Second Coming because He had just told His disciples in Matthew 24:29 exactly when He was going to return:

"Immediately after the tribulation of those days….."

When Jesus says no one can know the day of His coming, He must be speaking of the Rapture, and not the Second Coming.

2. THE DAY OF NOAH – VERSES 37-39
"But as the days of Noah were, so also will the coming of the Son of Man be. For as in the days before the flood, they were eating and drinking, marrying and giving in marriage, until the day that Noah entered the ark, and did not know until the flood came and took them all away, so also will the coming of the Son of Man be.

Note
Jesus says that when He returns, society will be like it was in the days of Noah when, up to the last moment, people were "eating and drinking" and "marrying and giving in marriage" – Matthew 24:38. In other words, life will continue as normal when He comes.

However, life would not be as normal during the Tribulation and Great Tribulation when at least half of the population of the world would have been killed. The Great Tribulation is not going to be a time of eating, drinking, marrying and giving in marriage as it is a period of great terror such as has never been since the beginning of the world nor ever shall be. Therefore, the period of eating, drinking and giving in marriage mentioned by Jesus can only refer to the period before the Rapture and not the Second Coming.

3. CATCHING UP - VERSES 40-41
"Then two men will be in the field: one will be taken and the other left. Two women will be grinding at the mill: one will be taken and the other left."

4. WATCHFULNESS – VERSES 42-44
"Watch therefore, for you do not know what hour your Lord is coming. But know this, that if the master of the house had known what hour the thief would come, he would have watched and not allowed his house to be broken into. Therefore you also be ready, for the Son of Man is coming at an hour you do not expect."

Note
The element of "watchfulness" is occasioned by the absence of warnings and signs before the actual event occurs. The seven-year events of the Tribulation and Great Tribulation would automatically remove the need to be watchful in the case of the Second Coming of Christ. Therefore, by elimination, watchfulness refers to the Rapture.

Furthermore, in Luke's account of the Olivet Discourse Luke quotes Jesus as saying:

"Watch therefore and pray always that you may be counted worthy to escape all these things that will come to pass and to stand before t h e Son of man" – **Luke 21:36**.

These words clearly refer to the Rapture.

5. FAITHFUL AND UNFAITHFUL SERVANTS
– MATTHEW 24 45-51

- The faithful servant expects his Master's arrival any moment – Verses 45-47.

- The unfaithful servant thinks his Master will delay His coming – **Verses 48-49.**

- "The Master of the servant will come on a day when he is not looking for him and at an hour that he is not aware of" – **Verse 50.**

The above analysis shows that the latter part of Matthew 24 describes the Rapture. We have sufficient biblical evidence pointing to a pre-tribulation rapture. Those who insist that the Rapture is not in view in the Olivet Discourse are doing more harm than good to the intent of the message of the text. The differences of opinion among theologians and Bible scholars have their roots not in the scriptures but rather in the assumptions made in the course of interpretation thereof. The fact that there is simply no scripture that explicitly states the timing of the Rapture should not be an excuse for adopting wrong assumptions leading to an erroneous conclusion that the Rapture takes place at the same time as the Second Coming.

Christ alludes to Rapture in His parable of the Ten Virgins in **Matthew 25:1-13**. At the conclusion of that parable, in verse 13, Jesus warns us to "watch" as we "know neither the day nor the hour in which the Son of Man is coming".

Let us contrast this with the fact that it will be possible for people to know the time of His Second Coming as all they have to do is to count seven years from the signing of the covenant the Antichrist makes with Israel which marks the beginning of Tribulation. However, no such prediction can be made about the Rapture.

All the foregoing arguments give credence to the pre-tribulation rapture view.

SECTION THREE
TRIBULATION AND GREAT TRIBULATION

This section gives a detailed and graphic account of the prophetic revelation of God's impending judgment to be unleashed upon the earth.

BOOK CHAPTER 11

TRIBULATION AND GREAT TRIBULATION

THE TRIBULATION PERIOD

- The Tribulation is a specific period of seven years of great distress and global calamity and disaster preceding the Second Coming of Jesus Christ.

- This period is divided into two equal segments of three and a half years each.

- The first period is known as the "Tribulation" while the second part is known as the "Great Tribulation".

- This seven-year period is revealed in **Daniel 9:24-27** (70th week) and fully described in great detail in **Revelation Chapters 6-19**. During this harrowing period, increasingly harsh and devastating judgements will be unleashed upon the world, starting with the "beginning of sorrows" (**Matthew 24:8**) and ending with the battle of Armageddon when the Lord defeats Satan and his armies.

It is practically impossible for human mind to fully comprehend and absorb the scale and enormity of the calamity to be released upon the unsuspecting world. All the end-time wars, rumours of war, famine and earthquake are but a mere preamble to the cataclysmic events of the tribulation period. Past and current events, especially the ongoing (at the time of compilation of this book) wave of pandemic, are all pointing to one fact – that we are inching closer and closer to the fulfilment of biblical prophecies. It would be wrong for anyone to assume or suggest that the current global economic and political upheavals coupled with the outbreak of pandemic, all amount to being in the Tribulation period. All these are periods of "contraction" and not the ultimate end-time events. ... ..."All these are the beginning of sorrows" – **Matthew 24:5-8**

In spite of all these experiences, men, by nature, have not learned their lessons but have chosen to ignore all the signs of the times.

BOOK CHAPTER 12

REVELATION CHAPTER 5

WHO IS WORTHY TO OPEN THE SCROLL AND BREAK THE SEALS?

REVELATION 5:1-7
And I saw in the right hand of Him who sat on the throne, a scroll written inside and on the back, sealed with seven seals. Then I saw a strong angel proclaiming with a loud voice, "Who is able to open the scroll, or to look at it?" So I wept much, because no one was found worthy to open and read the scroll, or to look at it. But one of the elders said to me, "Do not weep. Behold the lion of the tribe of Judah, the Root of David, has prevailed to open the scroll and to loose its seven seals." And I looked, and behold, in the midst of the throne and of the four living creatures, and in the midst of the elders, stood a Lamb as though it had been slain, having seven horns and seven eyes, which are the seven Spirits of God sent out into all the earth. Then He came and took the scroll out of the right hand of Him who sat on the throne.

After John had been plunged into boiling oil in Rome unscathed, he was banished to the Island of Patmos by Emperor Domitian about 95 AD all because of his unflinching faith in Christ. There he was shown the vision of future events and God's impending judgment upon the world.

In **chapter 5 of the Book of Revelation**, John sees in the right hand of God a scroll written on the front and on the back and sealed with seven seals. An angel makes a clarion call for anyone who is worthy to come forward to open the scroll and loose its seals. John bursts into tears because no one is found worthy. However, here comes a voice of hope from one of the elders to John: "Behold, the Lion of the tribe of Judah, the Root of David, has prevailed to open the scroll and to loose its seven seals."

The Scroll
Before books existed, scrolls were used to hold important information. In legal circles, legal deeds and legally binding agreements were held in a scroll.

The scroll in God's hand contains the terms for the redemption of the creation from the bondage and curse of sin. He has drawn this Will for the final settlement of the affairs of the universe. The earth has to be redeemed and returned to those who lost it through Adam in the garden of Eden. The contents are not only unchangeable, they are also divinely enforceable. In other words, they are judicial in nature and divine in content. The contents are so secret that the scroll had to be secured with seven seals.

The contents of this mysterious book define the rest of the book of Revelation and indeed provide the basis for understanding the programme of God for humanity.

The Seals
The scroll had been secured and authenticated by seven seals. The significance of the number of seals is profound. Under Roman law, a Will was always attested to by seven witnesses with seals which could only be opened when all seven witnesses or their legal representatives were present.

Jesus is here introduced as the "Lion of the Tribe of Judah" and the "Root of David." These double titles are very striking for the following reasons:

- His humanity is amplified by being the offspring of Judah
- His Deity is exemplified by His existence as the root and Creator of David.

The Lion and the Lamb

One of the elders introduces Jesus as the "Lion of the Tribe of Judah", but when John looked up, he sees, not a Lion, but a Lamb stepping forward to receive the scroll. Symbolically, the Lion and the Lamb respectively show the majesty and meekness of Christ. Meek when He came; majestic in His second coming. When Jesus came the first time, He came as a "Lamb of God" who suffered and died to take away the sins of the world. Then He was despised and rejected, but He is coming again as a Lion to destroy and avenge His enemies and establish His Kingdom and His Dominion which is from generation to generation.

Christ is inescapable. His presence is unavoidable. All men will meet Him either as a Redeemer and God's Lamb who died for their sins or as a Judge who comes to punish the unrepentant sinners. Do you want to meet Him as a Lamb or as a Lion? Today is the day of salvation when you can meet Christ as a Lamb of God. If you come to Him acknowledging your sins, you will receive His free gift of salvation. Anyone who rejects this offer now will certainly meet Him some day as a roaring Lion judging and punishing the ungodly.

BOOK CHAPTER 13

THE SEVEN SEALS AND THE SEVEN TRUMPETS

THE OPENING OF THE SEVEN SEALS

REVELATION CHAPTER 6

S E A L

Mysteries unfold as one by one the seals of the scroll are opened. Details of God's end time plans are being revealed. Time is closing in and God decides to release to mankind details of His impending judgment upon the earth. This is a fore warning from the Creator of heaven and earth because "the time is near".

Verses 1-8 detail the events and consequences of the four horses and their riders. Let us now examine these verses:

1ST SEAL - THE WHITE HORSE – Verses 1-2

"Now I saw when the Lamb opened one of the seals; and I heard one of the four living creatures saying with a voice like thunder, "Come and see." And I looked and behold a white horse. He who sat on it had a bow and a crown was given to him and he went out conquering and to conquer" – **NKJV.**

The white horse is a symbol of victory in war. The rider on the white horse here should not be confused with the rider in **Revelation 19:11** who is the victorious Christ called "Faithful and True."

The crown worn by the rider of the white horse in Revelation 6 is **"stephanos"** (in Greek), which is the victor's crown, whereas the crown worn by the rider of the white horse in **Revelation 19:11** is "diadem" (derived from Greek word "diadema") which means a Royal Crown.

Therefore, the rider in Revelation 6 is a military conqueror as he "had a bow and went out conquering and to conquer." He is a powerful world leader who promises false peace to the world. A Roman general would normally celebrate a triumph by parading on a white horse through the street. Hence the rider is seen riding a white horse as a symbol of victory.

The passage under consideration here depicts a catalogue of woe upon woe, war upon war and disaster upon disaster upon the world. The picture of this rider tells us the coming terror of the wrath of God.

2ᴺᴰ SEAL - THE RED HORSE – Verses 3-4

"When He opened the second seal, I heard the second living creature, saying "Come and See." Another horse, fiery red, went out. And it was granted to the one who sat on it to take peace from the earth, and that people should kill one another; and there was given to him a great sword." - **NKJV**

The red colour of this horse denotes bloodshed. The purpose of the red horse and its rider is to take away peace from the earth. The destructive tendency is to set man against man, nation against nation, kingdom against kingdom in a series of catastrophic conflicts resulting in global bloodshed. The earth will be plunged into the bloodiest war in human history.

This end-time vision is a vision of a time when all human relationships – national and international – will be destroyed and when hatred will pervade every political landscape.

3RD SEAL - THE BLACK HORSE (Verses 5-6)

"When He opened the third seal, I heard the third living creature say, "Come and see." So, I looked, and behold, a black horse, and he who sat on it had a pair of scales in his hand. And I heard a voice in the midst of the four living creatures saying, "A quart of wheat for a denarius; and three quarters of barley for a denarius; and do not harm the oil and the wine." - **NKJV**

The black horse and its rider stand for severe famine on a global scale. Food will be available but in short supply and at a prohibitive price. The food shortage will drive the price through the roof beyond what an average citizen can afford. A "denarius" was a day's wage in those times, with an equivalent purchasing power of £100 in today's value. This amount of money would barely feed a family for a day, with nothing left for other essentials of life. Curiously, wine and oil will not be affected as there will be abundant supply of those! Only the very rich will be able to afford a decent meal, leaving the masses suffering under the weight of extreme famine.

4TH SEAL - THE PALE HORSE – Verses 7-8

"When He opened the fourth seal, I heard the voice of the fourth living creature saying, "Come and see." So, I looked, and behold, a pale horse. And the name of him who sat on it was Death, and Hades followed with him. And power was given to them over a fourth of the earth, to kill with sword, with hunger, with death and by the beast of the earth." - NKJV

The weapons of destruction of the rider of the fourth horse are manifold:

- Sword
- Hunger
- mysterious death and
- Beasts

When God despatches His wrath upon the disobedient world through these multiple means, a quarter of the earth and its inhabitants will be destroyed. The pale horse and its rider bring famine, death and destruction upon the earth; as much as a fourth of the earth will be annihilated. This does not necessarily refer to a specific geographical area, but in all, a quarter of the earth and its population will be shattered. What a massive destruction affecting billions of people!

5TH SEAL - THE SOULS OF THE MARTYRS – Verses 9-11

"When He opened the fifth seal, I saw under the altar the souls of those who had been slain for the word of God and for the testimony which they held. And they cried with a loud voice, saying, "How long, O Lord, holy and true, until You judge and avenge our blood on those who dwell on the earth?" Then a white robe was given to each of them and it was said to them that they should rest a little while longer, until both the number of their fellow servants and their brethren, who would be killed as they were, was completed." **- NKJV**

At the opening of the fifth seal, comes the vision of the souls of those who had suffered persecution and died for their faith in Christ.

Who are these martyred saints? There have been many suggestions. A credible view is that these are the souls of the saints who will be slain during the tribulation period (after the Rapture of the Church) because of their faith in Christ. While their bodies await resurrection at the Second Coming of Christ, John saw their souls under the altar in heaven, indicating that they had sacrificed their lives as an act of worship to God through their witnessing and testimony of the Word of God. They are making passionate appeal for vengeance by crying with a loud voice. Just as the blood of Abel cried out for vengeance so does the blood of the martyrs. In **Genesis 4:10**, God said to Cain "What have you done? The voice of your brother's blood cries out to me from the ground."

Persecution can only kill the body and not the soul. Christ declared in **Matthew 10:28** – "Do not fear those who kill the body but cannot kill the soul. But rather fear Him who is able to destroy both soul and body in hell."

The cry for vengeance is a cry for justice. These saints have committed their cause to God – to whom vengeance belongs. "Vengeance is mine and I will repay, says the Lord." – **Romans 12:19.**

6TH SEAL - TERROR-STRICKEN UNIVERSE – Verses 12-17

"I looked when He opened the sixth seal, and behold, there was a great earthquake; and the sun became black as sackcloth of hair, and the moon became like blood. And the stars of heaven fell to the earth, as a fig tree drops its late figs when it is shaken by a mighty wind. Then the sky receded as a scroll when it is rolled up, and every mountain and island was moved out of its place.

And the kings of the earth, the great men, the rich men, the commanders, the mighty men, every slave and every free man, hid themselves in the caves and in the rocks of the mountains, and said to the mountains and rocks, "Fall on us and hide us from the face of Him who sits on the throne and from the wrath of the Lamb! For the great day of His wrath has come, and who is able to stand?" - **NKJV**

The opening of the sixth seal is followed by the following terrible events:
1. A great earthquake
Those who survived the ordeals of the previous seals will now face the devastation of the earthquake.

"The earth will quake and the heavens will tremble, the sun and moon will be darkened and stars grow dim" – **Joel 2:10.**

Such is the tide of destruction awaiting the earth and its inhabitants.

2. The darkened sun and faded moon
This event of the Day of the Lord is echoed by the following passages, among others:

- "For the stars of heaven and their constellations will not give their light, the sun will be darkened in its going forth and the moon will not cause its light to shine." – **Isaiah 13:10.**
- "The sun shall be turned into darkness, and the moon into blood before the coming of the great and awesome Day of the Lord" – **Joel 2:31.**
- "And it shall come to pass in that day, says the Lod God, That I will make the sun go down at noon. And I will darken the earth in broad daylight" – **Amos 8:9.**

3. The falling of the stars, The Folding up of the sky and The moving of the hills and island.
The galaxy and the firmament will be shaken. Here the prophecy of Isaiah is fulfilled:
"Therefore, I will shake the heavens and the earth will move out of her place. In the wrath of the Lord of hosts and in the day of His fierce anger." – **Isaiah 13:12**

The severity of these unprecedented events will throw the surviving population into a state of great panic, causing them to hide in the cave seeking protection from the wrath of God. Sin brings fear into man and drives man away from the presence of God. The corrupt world cannot withstand the wrath of God. Just as Adam did in the garden of Eden, the first instinct of a sinner is to hide from God. Sin brings a permanent separation from God. Sinful men will hide in the caves, pleading with the mountains and rocks to shield them from the wrath of God.

When the Day of the Lord comes, no one will be exempt from the judgment of God. All societal groups will be gripped with fear and run for cover. The seven groups mentioned in verse 15 are representative of the entire fabric of human society.

The kings
The great men
The rich
The commanders
The mighty men
Slaves
Free men

The significance of the seven listed groups is that the judgment of God is all-encompassing.

The Day of the Lord is further echoed by the following prophecies:

1. **Zephaniah 14**
2. **Joel 2:11**
3. **Hosea 10:8**

REVELATION CHAPTER 7

DIVINE PROTECTION
The Sealing of the Faithful

God offers special protection for the tribulation saints to be sealed before the emergence of the seven trumpets ushered in by the opening of the seventh seal in Revelation Chapter 8..

All in all, one hundred and forty four thousand of all the tribes of Israel

– twelve thousand from each tribe - will be sealed.

Revelation 7:5-8.
"And I heard the number of those who were sealed. One hundred and forty-four thousand of all the tribes of the children of Israel were sealed:"

Tribe of Judah	-12,000
Tribe of Reuben	-12,000
Tribe of Gad	-12,000
Tribe of Asher	-12,000
Tribe of Naphtali	-12,000
Tribe of Manasseh	-12,000
Tribe of Simeon	-12,000
Tribe of Levi	-12,000
Tribe of Issachar	-12,000
Tribe of Zebulun	-12,000
Tribe of Joseph	-12,000
Tribe of Benjamin	-12,000

After these, God shows John a great multitude of all nations who came out of the great tribulation standing before the throne, clothed with white robes and holding palm trees and singing a song of salvation unto God, serving Him day and night.

There have been different interpretations of the 144,000 saints. The Jehovah's Witnesses claim that this group represents a group of their founders and pioneers while others claim that the saints mentioned here are symbolic of the Church. However, both interpretations are wrong and misleading. **Revelation 7:4** clearly describes this group as coming from the tribe of the children of Israel, meticulously enumerating them by their tribes with 12,000 coming from each tribe. Clearly, these are Jewish evangelists that will be proclaiming the gospel during the Tribulation.

7TH SEAL – THE SEVEN TRUMPETS

REVELATION CHAPTER 8

THE OPENING OF THE SEVENTH SEAL
"When He opened the seventh seal, there was silence in heaven for about half and hour"- Verse 1.

The final assault and ultimate devastation of the earth is about to start. There is thirty minutes silence in heaven! This is no doubt the longest silence ever witnessed in heaven. It is unusual for heaven to be silent as the celestial realm is a place of continuous praise and worship. Nevertheless, the thirty minutes heavenly silence has brought the reality of the time of awesome expectation of what was about to be unleashed upon the unrepentant world.

THE SEVEN TRUMPETS
The opening of the seventh seal introduces the release of the seven trumpets.

1ST TRUMPET
(Verse 7)
Hail and blood destroyed a third of the trees and greens of the earth

2ND TRUMPET

(Verse 8)
A third of the sea became blood, leading to the demise of a third of the creatures in the sea and destruction of a third of the ships.

3RD TRUMPET

(Verses 9-11)
A star called Warmwood fell upon a third of the rivers and spring and they became bitter and many died from them.

4TH TRUMPET

(Verses 12-13)
A third of the sun, the moon and the stars were struck, and the earth became darkened.

REVELATION CHAPTER 9

5TH TRUMPET – THE BEGINNING OF WOES

(Verses 1-12)

1ST WOE – Bottomless Pit Opened and demonic locusts released
The angel of the Lord released deadly locusts from the bottomless pit headed by a terrible demon called Appolyon in Greek (Abbadon in Hebrew). They were commanded to torment for five months, but not kill, those who do not have the seal of God on their heads. In those days, the torment and agony will be so terrible that men would seek to die rather than remain alive. The shape of the locusts that John saw was like horses prepared for battle and their teeth were like lion's teeth and had tails like scorpions.

6TH TRUMPET

(Verses 13-21

2ND WOE – Four Angels of destruction were released.
The sixth angel releases the four angels bound at the river Euphrates and musters a great army numbering two hundred million (200,000,000) to kill a third of mankind with weapons of mass destruction. Sadly, in spite of this massive destruction, those who survive would refuse to repent of their evil deeds and acts of idolatry.

REVELATION CHAPTER 10

This chapter records the action of an angel making an announcement right from the presence of God that there should be delay no longer in unleashing the devastating judgment of the seventh trumpet. This is a divine announcement of the end. The scene is being set for the final showdown with the Antichrist and ultimate victory over the supreme monster of evil.

REVELATION CHAPTER 11

THE TWO WITNESSES
Before the seventh trumpets, verses 1-13 constitute the account of the two witnesses sent by God to prophesy for three and a half years.

These two unidentified witnesses were supernaturally protected while standing in Jerusalem to proclaim God and His Kingdom. Anyone who tries to obstruct them is consumed by fire from their mouth. They also have power to withhold rain and to strike the earth with plagues. Their appearance and activities set the stage for the seven-bowl judgements of God.

At the end of their prophetic mission, they will be murdered by the beast from the bottomless pit who is believed to be the same beast described in Revelation 13 otherwise known as the Antichrist. To the cynical world, this will seem like a major victory, claiming that their leader has finally defeated those who claim to speak for God. The euphoria of this seeming victory will lead to a celebration galore and exchange of gifts. The bodies of these witnesses will be left to rot in the streets. Their publicly displayed corpses will be beamed in real time to the global audience through the satellite news network.

However, after three and a half days, the joy of the world will be cut short when God miraculously resurrects these two witnesses in full glare of the world whose joy is turned into shock and horror. These two witnesses are then carried into heaven as the world gasp in awe.

The identity of the two witnesses
There are many views about the identity of the two witnesses. The two main theories are:
1. Moses and Elijah
This is because of the similarities of the miracles performed by the two witnesses to those performed by Moses and Elijah.
The two witnesses will have power to turn water into blood (**Revelation 11:6**) just as Moses turned water into blood in **Exodus 7.**
The two witnesses will have the power to destroy their enemies with fire just as Elijah called down fire in **2 Kings 1:10.**
Moses and Elijah appeared to Jesus at the Transfiguration (**Matthew 17:3**).

2. Enoch and Elijah
This is based on the unique circumstances surrounding their exit from the world without experiencing death (**Genesis 5:23; 2 Kings 2:11**).

The Scripture declares that it is appointed for men to die once (**Hebrews 9:27**). The fact that neither Enoch nor Elijah has experienced death seems to qualify them for the assignment of the two witnesses who will be killed after their assignment in order to fulfil the above Scripture

The identity of these witnesses is not an issue Christians should be dogmatic about. The most important element of this prophetic event is the proof that God is still in charge of the affairs of men and His awesome power of resurrection will ultimately be demonstrated as part of His final programme to defeat Satan.

7TH TRUMPET
(Verse 15)
3RD WOE

The sounding of the seventh trumpet is followed by loud voices in heaven acclaiming God's rulership and the reign of Christ over the kingdoms of this world. This acclamation is accompanied by a chorus of praises by the twenty-four elders, followed by thundering, lightning and earthquake.

REVELATION CHAPTER 12

Revelation chapter 12 is an interlude introducing the end of the great conflict between the Lord and Satan. It marks a concise history of Satan's efforts to thwart God's plan to save and bring humanity to Himself as part of His eternal family. Satan convinced a third of the angels to follow him in his attempt to make Himself like God, to deceive the entire world and to persecute God's people. This chapter provides an overview of history stretching from the pre-creation time until the time just before Christ's second return as King of kings and Lord of lords.

John saw a woman in heaven clothed with the sun, with the moon under her feet, and on her head a garland of twelve starts.

He also saw a dragon, with a third of the angels supporting him, standing before the woman who was ready to give birth, to devour her Child as soon as it was born.

The woman symbolises Israel.

In **Ezekiel 16**, God refers to His people as a woman whom He had dressed and adorned with ornament.

The garland of twelve stars on her head represent the twelve tribes of

Israel.

The Child stands for Jesus Christ.
According to verse 5, the male Child was to rule all nations with a rod of iron. Jesus Christ is the one who is prophesied to "strike the nations and rule them with a rod of iron" – Revelation 19:15

The dragon is none other than Satan
This dragon is clearly identified as Devil and Satan in verse **9 of Revelation 12**
Note verse 5 of the Chapter:
"She bore a male Child who was to rule all nations with a rod of iron. And her Child was caught up to God and His throne."
In **Isaiah 14:13-14,** the Bible gives us an insight into how Satan orchestrated a rebellion against God, attempting to exalt his throne above God's and be like the Most High.
The dragon standing before the woman, in order to devour the Child as soon as it was born, was a historical reference to King Herod's efforts to kill Jesus as a young child by ordering the killing of all male children from two years and under.

Although Satan's attempt to destroy Jesus when He was born failed, yet he did not give up his plan to forestall God's salvation programme. His frantic strategies of temptations and evil schemes during Christ's ministry failed to materialise. The dragon then became enraged with the woman and went to make war with the rest of her offspring – the body of Christ and true believers who overcame him by the blood of the Lamb and the word of their testimony.

BOOK CHAPTER 14

THE DRAGON, THE BEAST
(ANTICHRIST) AND THE FALSE PROPHET

REVELATION CHAPTER 13

After the interlude of chapter 12 comes the beginning of the Great Tribulation. We have a detailed description of three personalities:

1)   **The dragon**
      This is Satan cast out of heaven and having a little time.

2)   **The beast from the sea (The Antichrist)**
      This beast represents a political power (believed to be the revived Roman Empire)

3)   **The beast from the earth**
      This is a powerful religious figure and a false prophet.
      SATAN

Satan will make his great attempt to frustrate the programme of God by establishing his kingdom upon the earth. He will seek to achieve this by installing two great powers – one political and one religious. These are the two beasts mentioned in this chapter. The Beast from the Sea (Antichrist) represents satanic political powers while the Beast from the Earth (The False Prophet) is representative of the religious powers. The Beast from the Sea (The Antichrist)

"Then I stood on the sand of the sea. And I saw a beast rising up out of the sea, having seven heads and ten horns, and on his horns ten crowns, and on his heads a blasphemous name. Now the beast which I saw was like a leopard, his feet were like the feet of a bear, and his mouth like the mouth of a lion. The dragon gave him his power, his throne, and great authority. And I saw one of his heads as if it had been mortally wounded, and his deadly wound was healed. And all the world marveled and followed the beast. So, they worshiped the dragon who gave authority to the beast; and they worshiped the beast, saying 'Who is like the beast? Who is able to make war with him?' And he was given a mouth speaking great things and blasphemies, and he was given authority to continue for forty-two months." **Revelation 13: 1-5.**

The dragon gave his power, his throne and authority to this beast who will continue to exercise his delegated authority for forty-two months (three and a half years) – which is the duration of the Great Tribulation. Three characteristics are associated with this beast:
He will blaspheme the name of God
He will make war against the saints and overcome them
All who dwell on the earth, whose names are not written in the Lamb's book of life, will worship the beast.

The identity of the Antichrist
It is unwise to speculate about the identity of the Antichrist as his identity may not be known until the Church is taken away. Paul declares thus in 2 Thessalonians 2:3-4:
"Let no one deceive you by any means; for that Day will not come unless the falling away comes first and the man of sin is revealed, the son of perdition, who opposes and exalts himself above all that is called God or that is worshiped, so that he sits as God in the temple of God, showing himself that he is God."

Verses 11-17
The beast from the earth (The False Prophet)

This beast has two horns like a lamb but speaks like a dragon. This suggests a deceptive appearance. He has a meek appearance but a deadly disposition. He emerges as a powerful religious leader that claims to represent Christ but, in reality, is a messenger of Satan established to deceive the world by his miraculous signs. His characteristics include the following:

- He exercises all the authority of the first beast.
- He compels those who dwell on earth to worship the first beast.
- He performs great signs to deceive those on the earth.
- He forces all and sundry to receive the mark of the beast on their right hand or on their forehead.
- He ensures that anyone without the mark of the beast will not be able to buy or sell.

The Mark of the Beast
The number of the mark of the beast is 666.

Numerous and endless suggestions and permutations have been suggested as to the meaning of the number 666. Since it is the number of the beast, different individuals have come up with different interpretations to suit their arguments.
Everyone who pledges allegiance to the first beast will receive his mark on their hand or on their forehead. However, those who accept Christ will be sealed with the mark of life.

Has Covid-19 Vaccine Got Anything to Do with the Mark of the Beast?
There is some degree of reluctance among some Christians to take the Covid-19 vaccine based on the fear that the vaccine might be the mark of the beast.

There is no biblical evidence to link the Coronavirus pandemic to the prophetic narratives of the Tribulation Period. There is no correlation

THE RAPTURE AND THE SECOND COMING EXPLAINED

between the two for the following reasons:

- Whereas the prophetic plagues in the Book of Revelation are a direct action from God to punish the unrepentant world, the same cannot be said of the Coronavirus pandemic.
- Whilst Covid-19 vaccination is a scientific and medical programme to save lives, the mark of the beast is a cryptic mark to indicate allegiance to Satan.

REVELATION CHAPTER 14

THE SEAL OF CHRIST

In Revelation chapter 7, we encountered the sealing of one hundred and forty- four thousand servants of God who came from the twelve tribes of Israel, but chapter 14 tells us what the seal was. It was "His Father's Name". God will not bring His final judgment upon the earth until He has made safe those who belong to Him. These are the ones who are not defiled with women but follow the Lamb wherever He goes. They are the ones in whose mouth no falsehood is found. A true believer is simply one who lives an undefiled life and who follows Christ. In **John 1:43,** Jesus said to Philip and to the young ruler in **Mark 2:14** and to Levi, the tax collector, in **Mark 10:21,** "follow me."

A true follower of God must be a minister of the gospel with the responsibility of proclaiming to men and women the free gift of salvation and redemption through simple faith in Christ. A true believer is the one who receives the mark of Christ and refuses to get the mark of the beast.

This chapter portrays the life of a true follower of Christ as:
- A life of praise
- A life devoid of deceit and
- A life of gospel.

This chapter ends with the introduction of the Son of Man ready to thrust His sickle on the earth to reap His harvest. Therefore, the message of a true believer and messenger of God is not only a message of salvation to those who believe, but also a message of God's judgment awaiting those who reject Christ.

REVELATION CHAPTERS 15

This chapter marks an interlude presenting a picture of tribulation saints in heaven, who have not worshipped the beast, standing before the throne of God in rendition of worship songs reminiscent of the song that Moses sang after Israel's safe crossing of the Red Sea. These martyrs have emerged victorious from their conflict with the forces of Antichrist. To those who have laid their lives down on account of their faith in Christ, a day of persecution becomes a day of victory. Hence Jesus said: "whosoever loses his life for my sake will find it" – **Matthew 16:25.**

BOOK CHAPTER 15

THE SEVEN BOWLS OF GOD'S WRATH

BOWLS OF GOD'S WRATH

REVELATION CHAPTER 16

We are about to witness the final phase of God's wrath upon the earth. The pouring out of the seven bowls will mark the beginning of the latter part of God's judgment and culminate in the signaling of the return of Christ as recorded in **Revelation 19:11.**

Chapter 16 records the voice of God from the temple commanding the seven angels to "go and pour out the bowls of the wrath of God upon the earth". These bowls contain terrible plagues reminiscent of the ten plagues in Egypt.

Here comes the last terrible plagues poured out, one after the other, from the seven bowls of God's wrath:

THE RAPTURE AND THE SECOND COMING EXPLAINED

Verse 2
THE FIRST BOWL OF PLAGUE (Poured upon the Earth)

A foul and loathsome sore came upon the men who had the mark of the beast and those who worshiped his image.

Verse 3
THE SECOND BOWL OF PLAGUE (Poured upon the Sea)
The sea became blood and every living creature in it died.

Verses 4-6
THE THIRD BOWL OF PLAGUE (Poured upon the Rivers)
The rivers and springs became blood.

Verses 8-9
THE FOURTH BOWL OF PLAGUE
(Poured on the Sun)
Power was given to the sun to scorch men with fire and great heat. They blasphemed God and did not repent.

Verses 10-11
THE FIFTH BOWL OF PLAGUE
(Poured upon the throne of the Beast)
The evil kingdom of the beast was plagued with darkness and they gnawed their teeth because of pain and their sores but did not repent of their evil deeds.

Verses 12-14,16
THE SIXTH BOWL OF PLAGUE
(Poured upon river Euphrates)
The great river Euphrates was dried up making way for the invasion by the kings of the East (China and its allies). Demonic spirits will gather the kings of the earth to the battle of Armageddon.

Verses 17-20

THE SEVENTH BOWL OF PLAGUE
(Poured into the Air)
A great and unprecedented earthquake causing the great city to be split into three and the cities of the nations to crumble.

REVELATION CHAPTERS 17 AND 18

DIVINE JUDGMENT UPON THE GREAT HARLOT (BABYLON)

Chapter 17 reveals the great harlot (Babylon) controlling the economic and commercial powers of the world through her harlotry with the kings of the earth.

Babylon (the revived Roman Empire) is represented by a woman sitting on a scarlet beast, having seven heads and ten horns, drunk with the blood of saints and having in her hand a golden cup full of abomination and the filthiness of her fornication. The great harlot is judged because she corrupted the world. The worst of all sins is to teach others to sin. Her identification is shown on her forehead as: **MYSTERY, BABYLON THE GREAT, THE MOTHER OF HARLOTS AND OF THE ABOMINATION OF THE EARTH.**

Her seven heads represent seven kingdoms and her ten horns stand for ten kings who have received no kingdom.

Chapter 18 details the fall of Babylon. An angel with great authority made the announcement: "Babylon the great is fallen, is fallen, and has become a dwelling place of demons, a prison for every foul spirit, and a cage for every unclean and hated bird! For all the nations have drunk of the wine of the wrath of her fornication, the kings of the earth have committed fornication with her, and the merchants of the earth have become rich through the abundance of her luxury." – verses 2 and 3.

THE RAPTURE AND THE SECOND COMING EXPLAINED

God steps in to judge human arrogance and rebellion. Babylon is punished by God for her immorality and corruption. Within one hour, Christ completely crushes the haughty and corrupt Babylon, grinding her to dust, and the kings and merchants of the earth who were deceived and corrupted by her weep and lament for her, while they watch in horror the scale of her destruction. The perpetrator of iniquity will be gone and shall not be found anymore! God will finally avenge His people. Hence the chorus in **verse 20: "Rejoice over her, O heaven and you holy apostles and prophets, for God has avenged you on her!"**

SECTION FOUR
THE SECOND COMING OF CHRIST

BOOK CHAPTER 16

THE WEDDING OF THE LAMB

(REVELATION 19:7 - 10)

THE WEDDING OF THE LAMB
"Let us be glad and rejoice and give Him glory, for the marriage of the Lamb has come, and His wife has made herself ready. And to her it was granted to be arrayed in fine linen, clean and bright, for the fine linen is the righteous acts of the saints. Then he said to me, 'Write: Blessed are those who are called to the marriage supper of the Lamb!' And he said to me, 'These are the true sayings of God.' And I fell at his feet to worship him. But he said to me, 'See that you do not do that! I am your fellow servant, and of your brethren who have the testimony of Jesus. Worship God! For the testimony of Jesus is the spirit of prophecy.'" – **Revelation 19:7-10.**

By the time we get to chapter 19, we have come to the end of the Tribulation Period. Just before the beginning of the Tribulation, the Church will be raptured to be with the Lord, and immediately after the Tribulation, she will return to the earth with Christ. In other words, the Rapture and the Second Coming of Christ are on either side of the Tribulation period. The controversy thrown up by opposing views has been comprehensively discussed in **SECTION 3** of this book.

Verses 1-6

This chapter begins with a shout of great multitude in heaven jubilating over God's judgment upon the great harlot who has deceived and corrupted the earth. The shout is Hallelujah which means "Praise the Lord." God is praised because salvation, glory and honour belong to Him. The constituent elements of real praise are gratitude and reverence.

The wedding of the Lamb (Christ) with his bride (the Church) will take place in heaven before Christ comes back to judge the world and reign on earth with His saints. Heaven rejoices because:

- The marriage of the Lamb is come.
- His wife has made herself ready.
- She is arrayed in fine line, clean and white, depicting her righteousness.

REVELATION CHAPTER 19: 11 - 21

Now I saw heaven opened, and behold, a white horse. And He who sat on him was called Faithful and True, and in righteousness He judges and makes war. His eyes were like a flame of fire, and on His head were many crowns. He had a name written that no one knew except Himself. He was clothed with a robe dipped in blood, and His name is called The Word of God. And the armies in heaven, clothed in fine linen, white and clean, followed Him on white horses. Now out of His mouth goes a sharp sword, that with it He should strike the nations. And He Himself will rule them with a rod of iron. He Himself treads the winepress of the fierceness and wrath of Almighty God. And He has on His robe and on His thigh a name written: **KING OF KINGS AND LORD OF LORDS**. Then I saw an angel standing in the sun, and he cried with a loud voice, saying to all the birds that fly in the midst of heaven, "Come and gather together for the supper of the great God, that you may eat the flesh of kings, the flesh of captains, the flesh of mighty men, the flesh of horses and of those who sit on them, and the flesh of all people, free and slave, both small and great." And I saw the beast, the kings of the earth, and their armies, gathered together, to make war against Him who sat on the horse and against His army. Then the beast was captured, and with him the false prophet who worked signs in his presence, by which he deceived those who received the mark of the beast and those who worshiped his image. These two were cast alive into the lake of fire burning with brimstone. And the rest were killed with the sword which proceeded from the mouth of Him who sat on the horse. And all the birds were filled with their flesh.

BOOK CHAPTER 17

THE RETURN OF CHRIST AND THE BINDING OF SATAN

The Second Coming refers to Christ's return to earth immediately after the Great Tribulation. His return will be literal, physical and visible.

A Rider on a White Horse

John sees before him an open heaven and a white horse with a rider unmistakably identified as Faithful and True.

- His eyes are like a flame of fire denoting the fact that nothing is hidden from Him.

- On His head are many crowns, symbolizing His Majesty.

- He is clothed in a robe dipped in blood emblematic of His victory over Satan.

Here comes one of the most dramatic moments in the book of Revelation and in human history – the coming of the conquering Christ. He who once came as a meek and gentle lamb now emerges as a conquering King, a fearful Judge and a Royal Commander followed by His unconquerable army on a mission to smash his enemies, judge the ungodly world and establish His Kingdom on earth. His Kingdom will be an everlasting Kingdom and His dominion is from generation to generation.

It is extremely important to distinguish the Rapture from the Second Coming of Christ. This Second Advent will be in two phases. First, He will come to take His bride (the Church) out of this world. This event is called the Rapture. This will be a secret coming "like a thief in the night." The second phase is when He comes back to earth with His bride (armies) as recorded in Revelation 19:14. This will be public event when all eyes shall see Him.

The Second Coming of Christ marks the climax not only of the book of Revelation but also the entire Bible. Over the years, prophets have been eagerly looking forward to this event and expectant believers have been prayerfully waiting for this moment to come. "Thy Kingdom Come" has always been the thematic prayer of the faithful. Here comes the answer to the disciples' prayer.

The dominant hope of all true believers is the appearing of the Lord and we eagerly long for His coming to take us home so that where He is, we may be also.

THE CAPTURE OF THE BEAST
(Revelation 19:19-21)
At the Second Advent of Christ, the beast from the sea (the antichrist) and the beast from the earth (the false prophet) will be captured and thrown into the lake of fire. The terrible reign and the diabolical activities of the antichrist will come to an end. The evil will be utterly terminated, and the troublers of the world will be completely exterminated. These two beasts have been prosecuting the agenda of Satan through the persecution of the Tribulation saints. Suddenly, their end will come, and they will spend eternity in the lake of fire. The evil of this world can thrive only for a while, but the conquering Christ, Faithful and Just, has the final say.

A recap of the Activities of the Antichrist
In order to fully appreciate the significance of the victory over the two beasts, it is necessary to sum up the activities of the antichrist during

the seven-year period of Tribulation and Great Tribulation.

As earlier mentioned, the beast from the sea is the antichrist while the beast from the earth is the false prophet. The antichrist is otherwise known as the man of sin/lawlessness (2 Thessalonians 2:3) or the lawless one (2 Thessalonians 2:8,9). The false prophet operates on behalf of the antichrist who, in turn, is Satan's agent. The antichrist has the following master strategies:

1. Signing and Breaking of Covenant with Israel
At the beginning of the tribulation period, the antichrist signs a seven-year covenant with Israel which guarantees her safety and protection. This will encourage disarmament on the part of Israel leading to redirection of resources from military to economic development. The covenant will lead to the building of the third Temple and restoration of sacrifice and offering. However, the antichrist will break the covenant half-way through the seven-year period (Daniel 9:27). He will suspend Temple sacrifice and offering and bring abomination by entering the Temple and establishing himself as one to be worshipped.

2. He exalts himself
"Then the king shall do according to his own will: he shall exalt and magnify himself above every god, shall speak blasphemies against the God of gods, and shall prosper till the wrath has been accomplished; for what has been determined shall be done. He shall regard neither the God of his fathers nor the desire of women, nor regard any god; for he shall exalt himself above them all." – **Daniel 11:36-37**

"Who opposes and exalts himself above all that is called God or that is worshiped, so that he sits as God in the temple of God, showing himself that he is God". – **2 Thessalonians 2:4.**

The antichrist exhibits the power of sin, pride, arrogance and self-righteousness in his desire to exalt himself above God and His will.

Here, however, is the good news. **2 Thessalonians 2:8** declares that the man of sin will be crushed and consumed by Christ with the breath of His mouth and the brightness of His coming. Hallelujah!

3. He gains global political and military dominance

The antichrist will seek to gain global political and military dominance –

"At the time of the end the king of the South shall attack him; and the king of the North shall come against him like a whirlwind, with chariots, horsemen, and with many ships; and he shall enter the countries, overwhelm them and pass through. He shall also enter the Glorious Land, and many countries shall be overthrown; ….He shall stretch out his hand against the countries and the land of Egypt shall not escape." – **Daniel 11:40-42.**

4. He controls the world economy

"He shall have power over the treasures of gold and silver, and over all the precious things of Egypt; Also the Libyans and Ethiopians shall follow at his heels" – **Daniel 11:43**

5. He seeks to control the world religion

He uses the second beast (the false prophet) to advance his religious supremacy. **In Revelation Chapter 13** from verse 11 onwards, the second beast appears on the scene and exercises all the authority of the first beast and causes the earth and those who dwell in it to worship the first beast. He performs great signs, so that he even makes the fire come down from heaven in the sight of men and deceives those who dwell on the earth by those signs and wonders.

6. He makes himself an object of worship

The second beast compels those who dwell on the earth to make and worship the image of the first beast. – Revelation 13:4-6; 8; 14.

7. He makes war with the saints

"It was granted to him to make war with the saints and to overcome

them, and authority was given him over every tribe tongue and nation" – **Revelation 13:7.**
"He shall speak pompous words against the Most High; Shall persecute the saints of the Most High" – **Daniel 7:25.**

The antichrist will make the tribulation saints his personal target, subjecting them to severe oppression and persecution. Many will be killed for their faith in Christ and their refusal to worship the image of the beast. Much as he tries, he will be unable to destroy their faith or fully exterminate them. Even today, Christians in some parts of the world are being persecuted for their faith in Christ but "Who shall separate us from the love of Christ? Shall tribulation, or distress, or persecution, or famine, or nakedness, or peril, or sword? For I am persuaded that neither death nor life, nor angels nor principalities nor powers nor things present, nor things to come, nor height nor depth, nor any other created thing, shall be able to separate us from the love of God which is in Christ Jesus our Lord" (**Romans 8:35, 38, 39**)

8. He forces everyone to receive his mark – 666
9. He will be consumed by Christ

THE BINDING OF SATAN
(Revelation 20:1-3)
"Then I saw an angel coming down from heaven, having the key to the bottomless pit and a great chain in his hand. He laid hold of the dragon, that serpent of old, who is the Devil and Satan, and bound him for a thousand years, and he cast him into the bottomless pit, and shut him up and set a seal on him so that he should deceive the nations no more till the thousand years were finished. But after these things, he must be released for a little while."

Satan, the prince and troubler of the world, the accuser of brethren, the deceiver, the old dragon, the principal ruler of the darkness of this world, has now come to the end of his reign. The one that has always regarded himself as invisible, untouchable and unreachable now meets his waterloo when an angel of the Living God, coming from heaven with great authority and having the key to the bottomless pit and a chain in his hand, apprehends him with no force whatsoever, binds him and throws him into the bottomless pit and shuts him up for a thousand years. The devil himself knows that his time is short as declared in **Revelation 12:12 "Therefore, rejoice, O heavens, and you who dwell in them, but woe to you O earth and sea for the devil has come down to you in great wrath because he knows that his time is short."**

What a huge relief for the inhabitants of the world enjoying a thousand years of peace! Can you imagine a life where Satan isn't around to trouble and deceive people? The abyss or bottomless pit is a place of confinement where Satan will be kept for one thousand years pending his final sentencing to a lake of fire.

BOOK CHAPTER 18

THE MILLENNIUM, JUDGMENTS AND FINAL JUDGEMENTS

THE MILLENNIUM

Millennium refers to one thousand years of Christ's reign on earth. The word comes from the Latin word "Mille" which means one thousand, and "annum" which stands for year. This will be a period of great peace and prosperity as Satan will be bound throughout the entire period and unable to deceive the world. Even the wild animals will be of good behaviour in the Millennium, and nothing will be harmful to the inhabitants of the earth.

Isaiah 11:6-9
"The wolf also shall dwell with the lamb, the leopard shall lie down with the young goat, the calf and the young lion and the fatling together; And the lion shall eat straw like the ox. The nursing child shall play by the cobra's hole, and the weaned child shall put his hand in the viper's den."

Isaiah 65:25
"The wolf and the lamb shall feed together, the lion shall eat straw like the ox, and the dust shall be the serpent's food. They shall not hurt nor destroy in all My holy mountain, says the Lord."

The length of the Millennium is literally one thousand years as stated six times in **Revelation 20:2-7**. Some people erroneously believe the one thousand-year period of Millennium to be figurative or symbolic.

After the Millennium, God will release Satan from prison. The devil in his folly will try and fight Jesus one more time to take control of the universe, but he will be defeated and completely exterminated. Ultimately, Satan, the devil and our adversary will be thrown into the lake of fire and brimstone, where the beast and the false prophet are, and they will be tormented day and night forever and ever.!

The Timing of the Millennium

Now that we have established the length of the millennium as literally one thousand years, it is helpful to know that there are three main views about its timing. This will help dispel any confusion surrounding this topic. These views are:

1. Amillennial View of the Millennium (Amillennialism)

This view does not believe in a future millennium. It believes that Christ's reign in the millennium is not a bodily reign here on earth but rather the heavenly reign which is already taking place and Christians who have died are already partaking in that reign. In essence, this position believes that the millennium mentioned in Revelation 20 is currently being fulfilled in the present Church age.

Author's Comments

I consider this view to be untenable and without any biblical basis.

2. Postmillennial View of the Millennium (Postmillennialism)

This position believes that Christ will return after the millennium and that the progressive expansion of the gospel will eventually result in a millennial age of peace and righteousness on the earth. This view further believes that the millennium is not necessarily a literal period of one thousand years. The proponents of this view believe that Christ will return to earth at the end of this period. This view was prevalent when the Church was experiencing great revival with the absence of war and international conflict.

3. Premillennial view of the Millennium (Premillennialism)
This view holds that Christ will come back before the millennium. This
viewpoint has a clear and solid biblical basis and has a long historical
support from the earliest centuries. This position is confirmed by the
following biblical facts:

Christ's Second Coming occurs immediately after the Great Tribulation
– **Matthew 24:29-30**
Christ's Return occurs first – **Revelation 19**
The Millennium follows – **Revelation 20.**

Satan Released After One Thousand Years – Revelation 20:7-10

Satan will again display his stubbornness following his release from one thousand years imprisonment. This shows that Satan will never have any remorse for his wrongdoings as he is beyond reformation and redemption. Even in his incarceration, he is still under the illusion that he stands a chance in fighting Christ. However, his delusion is short-lived.

On his release, he resumes his campaign of deception to the nations of the earth. We should bear in mind that up until his release, the whole world will enjoy peace and prosperity in his absence. His reappearance on the stage will interrupt this peaceful and harmonious human coexistence. He tries to convince the nations of the world to gather in battle against God and His Christ. These powerful nations respond without a second thought, resulting in a coalition of a huge army whose number is as the sand of the sea. Two names are specifically mentioned – **Gog and Magog.**

Gog and Magog
Different scholars have put forward contrasting views about the identity of Gog and Magog. Without delving too much into the different views, Gog is commonly believed to represent a tyrannical leader (linked to Iran) while Magog, according to some scholars, refers to Russia and republic of the former Soviet Union. However, others believe that the word Magog may simply be a generalization for an end-time archenemy of Israel without a specific location. Some bible commentators even suggest a link between Gog and Magog mentioned in Ezekiel Chapters 38 and 39 and Gog ad Magog of Revelation 20.

Considering all the available evidence and interpretations, it is realistic to say that the prophetic reference to Gog and Magog in this chapter of Revelation refers to a coalition of powerful countries, probably Russia, Iran, China, Turkey and other allies. Satan in his deception will galvanize a massive military alliance to fight this war. Reference to "the nations in the four corners of the earth" implies that other countries may be involved, not least Syria, Lebanon, Libya etc.

JUDGEMENT

(REVALATION 20:4 - 6; 11 - 15)

Several scripture passages speak about the coming judgments. Different judgments will take place at different times:

BEMA SEAT JUDGMENT
2 Corinthians 5:10
"For we must all appear before the judgment seat of Christ, that each one may receive the things done in the body, according to what he has done, whether good or bad.
Romans 14:10
"....For we shall all stand before the judgment seat of Christ. "

It is believed that this judgment is to reward true believers who have been raptured.

TRIBULATION SAINTS AND
OLD TESTAMENT SAINTS JUDGMENT

Revelation 20:4-6
"And I saw thrones, and they sat on them, and judgment was committed to them. Then I saw the souls of those who had been beheaded for their witness to Jesus and for the word of God, and those who had not worshiped the beast or his image, and had not received his mark on their foreheads or on their hands. And they lived and reigned with Christ for a thousand years. But the rest of the dead did not live again until the thousand years were finished. This is the first resurrection. Blessed and holy is he who has part in the first resurrection. Over such the second death has no power but they shall be priest of God and of Christ, and shall reign with Him a thousand years."
Daniel 2:2
"And many of those who sleep in the dust of the earth shall awake,

some to everlasting life and some to shame and everlasting contempt."

JUDGMENT OF UNBELIEVERS OF ALL TIMES
At the end of the Millennium, unbelievers of all times will be raised and judged before the Great White Throne.
Revelation 20:11-15
"Then I saw a great white throne and Him who sat on it, from whose face the earth and the heaven fled away. And there was found no place for them. And I saw the dead, small and great, standing before God, and books were opened. And another book was opened which is the Book of Life. And the dead were judged according to their works, by the things which were written in the books. The sea gave up the dead who were in it, and Death and Hades delivered up the dead who were in them. And they were judged, each one according to his works. Then Death and Hades were cast into the lake of fire. This is the second death. And anyone not found written in the Book of Life was cast into the lake of fire."

THE JUDGE
In all these judgements, Christ will be the judge as the Scripture declares in **John 5:22** "For the Father judges no one, but has committed all judgment to the Son.

It is high time the world accepts Jesus Christ as the Lord and Saviour before whom every soul will appear to be judged.

Author's Comments
The doctrine of Judgements and the Final Judgment should give us:
1. the assurance of ultimate divine justice
2. the encouragement to mend our ways and forgive others freely
3. the motivation to pursue righteousness and
4. the impetus for evangelism.

BOOK CHAPTER 19

THE NEW HEAVEN,
THE NEW EARTH AND THE ETERNAL KINGDOM

(REVELATION CHAPTER 21)

REVELATION 21:1-3
"Now I saw a new heaven and a new earth, for the first heaven and the first earth had passed away. Also there was no more sea. Then I, John, saw the holy city, New Jerusalem, coming down out of the heaven from God, prepared as a bride adorned for her husband., And I heard a loud voice from heaven saying 'Behold, the tabernacle of God is with men, and He will dwell with them, and they shall be His people. God Himself will be with them and be their God.'"

ISAIAH 65:17-18
For behold, I create new heavens and a new earth; And the former shall not be remembered or come to mind. But be glad and rejoice forever in what I create; For behold, I create Jerusalem as a rejoicing, and her people a joy."

After the final judgment, believers will enter the presence of God in a renewed creation – a new heaven and a new earth. God will cause His tabernacle to be with His saints where He will dwell with them and there shall no more be death or anything accursed, no more weeping nor crying – **Isaiah 65:19.**

In **Isaiah 65:17**, God promises to create new heavens and a new earth. Hence Apostle Peter reminds us of the need to "look for new heavens and a new earth in which righteousness dwells" – **2 Peter 3:13.**

Here in **Revelation 21**, John sees a vision of heaven and earth unified in the Holy City, "new Jerusalem," coming down out of heaven from God, prepared as a bride adorned for her husband, denoting the manifestation of the impeccable Kingdom where we will live in the presence of God forever. Hence Jesus says "Come O blessed of my Father, inherit the Kingdom prepared for you from the foundation of the world – **Matthew 25:34.**

"And God will wipe away every tear from their eyes; there shall be no more death, nor sorrow, nor crying. There shall be no more pain, for the former things have passed away" - **Revelation 21:4.**

In this Kingdom we will be free from pain, sorrow and suffering, and, more importantly, we will continually enjoy unhindered fellowship with our Lord and King.

The account of the new heaven and the new earth should give us a strong motivation for godly living and for storing up our treasures in heaven, where moth and rust do not corrupt as explicitly instructed in **Matthew 6:20.**

We are enjoined to enter God's Kingdom only through the narrow gate because the highway to hell is broad and its gate is wide for the many who throng it. We must strive to enter the new heaven and the new earth – the tabernacle of God where He will be with us and be our God. He who sits on the throne and who makes all things new declares to John in **Revelation 21:6-7:**

"It is done! I am the Alpha and the Omega, the Beginning and the End. I will give of the fountain of the water of life freely to him who thirsts. He who overcomes shall inherit all things, and I will be his God and he shall be My son."

This means Christ has done it all for us. Hallelujah!

Also found in this chapter are classes of characters and various categories of people who cannot find a place in the Holy City. We have eight categories:

1. The Cowardly
Cowardice is a spirit which makes man to deny Christ in times of adversity. The cowardly sinks into the mire of doubt and fear. As Peter denied Jesus three times in his time of distress, many Christians would deny their faith in Christ when troubles befall them. These are believers who deny Christ for the fear of losing their lives. Because Christ has shared our pain, His mercy is available to rescue us from sinking when battered by the waves of fear. He rescued Peter, and He can rescue us in times of adversity. Great were the courage and boldness exhibited by those before us who were not mindful of their lives but boldly affirmed their faith in Christ even when in the midst of their persecution they came face to face with roaring hungry lions.

"But whoever denies me before man, him I will also deny before My Father who is in heavens" – **Matthew 10:33.**

2. The Unbelieving
The unbelieving are those who lack the sincere faith of the gospel; those who deny their faith in Christ.
"Whoever believes in Him is not condemned, but whoever does not believe has already been condemned because he has not believed in the name of the only begotten Son of God" – **John 3:18.**

"He who believes in the Son has everlasting life; and he who does not believe the Son shall not see life, but the wrath of God abides on him" – John 3:36

3. The Abominable

These are people whose conduct is offensive to God; those who wallow in their sins and have become detestable to God.

"For this reason, God gave them up to vile passions. For even their women exchanged the natural use for what is against nature. Likewise, also the men, leaving the natural use of the woman, burned in their lust for one another, men with men committing what is shameful, and receiving in themselves the penalty of their error which was due – Romans 1:26-27.

"You shall not lie with a male as with a woman. It is an abomination. Nor shall you mate with any animal, to defile yourself with it. Nor shall any woman stand before an animal to mate with it. It Is perversion. Do not defile yourselves with any of these things; for by all these the nations are defiled, which I am casting out before you." Leviticus 18:22-24

4. Murderers

Murder is undoubtedly one of the most gruesome sin. Life is the most precious and irreplaceable thing. Murder can occur in many ways:

- Physically killing another person - Cain
- Plotting another person's death - Jezebel
- Maligning and wishing evil against someone
- Consenting to another person's death – Paul
- Failure to prevent another person's death when it is within one's power.
- Taking away other people's means of livelihood or life support.
- By witchcraft or sorcery.
- Whosoever hates his brother is a murderer – **1 John 3:15**

No murderer will go unpunished. It is frightening to learn that hatred towards one's brother is murder. Many Christians may still be living in this dangerous territory. However, God is merciful, if we repent of our sins, He will forgive us. Today is the day of repentance and salvation.

Do not procrastinate.

5. Sexually Immoral
These include whoremongers, people who defile their neighbours' wives, commit other sexual immoralities or indulge in lusts, lewdness and uncleanness.

6. Sorcerers
Conjurers and those who get involved in sorcery, witchcraft, fetish practices and other demonic activities

7. Idolaters
Idolatry is one of the practices listed in Galatians 5:20 that would make people not to enter the Kingdom of God. Idolatry is the worship of an idol or a physical image such as a statue or a person in place of God. Idol worship takes various forms in our modern day. A person, situation, circumstance or substance can be turned into an idol. This happens when we place the value on that person, thing or situation over our value for God. In other words, anything you consider to be more important to you than God. Is any individual more important to you than God? Is silver and gold more important to you than God? Are the glitters of this world more important to you than God? Is fame or position more important to you than God? Think about any set of circumstances in your life that could be placed over and above God and which could make you drift away from Him. The aggressive and ungodly pursuit of money and wealth has all the hallmarks of idolatry.

8. Liars
Satan is not only a liar but the father of lies. Those who speak what they know to be false, including hypocrites, will be guilty before God.

Liars are people who cannot be trusted. Those who are false in their dealings, in their statements and in their promises towards man and God. A true Christian must never be listed among liars because such shall have their part in the lake which burns with fire and brimstone.

WARNING!

Those who fall in any of the above categories have one thing in common – they shall have their part in the lake which burns with fire and brimstone. This should give every reader of this book food for thought.

CHAPTER 20

EPILOGUE

THE RAPTURE AND THE SECOND COMING OF CHRIST

In the preceding chapters of this book, we established the fact that The Second Coming of Christ is one of the most momentous events in human history and this doctrine is at the forefront of contemporary theological debate among Christians and Bible scholars. The Bible provides clear and detailed teachings concerning the future programme of God culminating in the Second Advent of Christ to judge the world and reward His saints.

The Scripture is our source of knowledge of prophecy and the constant study of the Word of God provides joy in the midst of affliction, hope in the midst of uncertainties and strength in a weary land.

So far, we have considered the various views concerning the nature and the timing of the Second Coming of Christ. For clarity, it is helpful to recall the following sequence of exposition:
   1) The Rapture
   2) Tribulation and Great Tribulation.
   3) The Second Coming of Christ.

THE TWO PHASES OF CHRIST'S SECOND COMING
There is a tremendous amount of debate over the doctrine of Rapture. Many believers and students of Bible prophecy find it a bit confusing that our Lord's Second Coming will be in two phases. The first phase

THE RAPTURE

The word "Rapture" is derived from the Latin word "Rapturo" and Greek word **"Harpazo"** which is translated **"snatched up"** or **"caught up."**

Although the word "rapture" is not explicitly used in the New Testament, there exist a lot of references to the doctrine. In fact, there are other words like "trinity", "the Lord's prayer" that are taught in Scripture even though the exact words were not used.

There is universal unanimity of opinion on the doctrine of rapture, but there exists a substantial divergence of opinion on the timing. The differences of opinion on this aspect of Bible prophecy have degenerated into a state of intransigence among Bible scholars and apathy among Christians at large. Whatever the case may be, our doctrinal disagreement must not be a cause for division among believers. Let us now consider the three main views on this doctrine:

1) Pre-tribulation Rapture View

This view holds that the Rapture will occur before the start of the seven-year Tribulation Period at the end of which Jesus Christ will come back to earth. This view holds that the Church will   not experience the wrath of God that will be unleashed upon the earth during the Tribulation.

The Rapture is for those who are in Christ, and it relates exclusively to the Church Age. Church Age believers are resurrected and raptured before the Tribulation whereas the resurrection at the end of Tribulation relates to the Tribulation martyrs and not Church Age believers. According to Revelation 19:14, when Christ returns, He comes with the armies of heaven. The plural word   "armies" denotes two companies of army – the angelic army and the Church army who had been raptured before the Tribulation.

Author's Comments

The pre-tribulation rapture theory is the only theory that harmonises Scriptures and correctly applies literal-grammatical- historical method of interpretation of end-time prophecies.

2) Mid-tribulation Rapture View

This view believes that the Rapture will occur at the mid-point of the seven-year Tribulation Period. This places three and a half years between the Rapture of the Church and the Second Coming of Christ.

Author's Comments

There are fundamental problems with this view.

- The first problem is the belief that the Church will experience the first half of the tribulation period just before the Great Tribulation. In other words, the Church will go through the serious wrath of God in the first half of the Tribulation but will escape the more serious wrath of the second half. This view is completely contradictory to the rest of the Bible, as nowhere has God poured out His wrath on the righteous. Furthermore, the Scriptures tell us in 1 Thessalonians 5:9 that the Church is not destined to wrath.

- The second problem with this view is that it tends to say that the "last" trumpets mentioned in 1 Corinthians 15:52, Matthew 24:31 and 1 Thessalonians 4:16 are the same as the "seventh" trumpet mentioned in Revelation 11:15. The truth is that the "seventh" trumpet call of Revelation 11:15 is the last in a series of seven trumpets but not the same as the last trumpet announcing the commencement of Christ's kingdom in Matthew 24:31 nor the trumpet call of God to gather His elect in 1 Thessalonians 4:16.

In a nutshell, the mid-tribulation rapture view is without biblical foundation.

3) Post-tribulation Rapture View

The post-tribulation rapture position teaches that the Rapture will occur at the end of the seven-year Tribulation period and that the

Church will be on earth during this period. In other words, the Church will not be raptured before the Tribulation, but pass through the Tribulation and that only when Christ returns at the end of the Tribulation will the Church be caught up.

It also believes that the Rapture and the Second Coming of Christ will happen simultaneously. According to that theory, when believers are raptured to meet Christ in the air, He will immediately make a U-turn back to earth together with them.

Author's Comments
This view is flawed for the following reasons, among others:
- There is no biblical support for the suggestion that Christ will receive the Church in the air and then make an immediate U-turn back to earth.
- It tends to ignore the biblical fact that many signs will precede the Second Coming while no signs whatsoever will precede the Rapture.
- Posttribulationalism has completely overlooked Christ's promise to go and prepare a place for us in His Father's house and come back to receive us to Himself so that where He is, there we may also be.
- The suggestion that the Church will experience the Tribulation is unbiblical as many Bible passages indicate that the Church is not destined for God's wrath.
- If there was a post-tribulation rapture, every saved person on earth would have a resurrection body and there would be no one to populate the millennial Kingdom as, according to Jesus, "in the resurrection they neither marry nor are given in marriage but are like angels of God in heaven" – Matthew 22:30.

COMPARATIVE MERITS OF PRE-TRIB RAPTURE VIEW
The two most prominent contrasting views in the contemporary debates about the timing of the Rapture are:
1) Pre-tribulation rapture view and

2) Post-tribulation rapture view.

While pre-tribulation rapture scholars believe that the Rapture will occur before the seven-year tribulation period, the post-tribulation scholars advocate that the Church will continue on earth during the entirety of the seven-year tribulation after which there will be a Rapture, followed immediately by the Second Coming of Christ.

The proponents of post-tribulation rapture view base their arguments principally on the following historical and theological premises:

1) Historical premise
The pre-tribulation rapture view is always viewed as a relatively new doctrine.

Author's Response
Although the spread of pre-tribulation rapture view is relatively new, it doesn't mean it is wrong. In fact, early Christian fathers had always believed in this doctrine despite the fact that it only started gaining ground during the turn of nineteenth century.

2) Theological premise
Another argument often put forward by post-tribulationists is that a two-phase pre-tribulation Rapture is never mentioned in the Bible.
Author's Response
This argument is self-defeating because the Bible does not explicitly or implicitly mention anywhere that the rapture will occur after the Tribulation. In fact a careful study of Scripture reveals that the Bible teaches pre-tribulation Rapture which has in turn been affirmed and adequately explained by scores of respected Bible scholars and seasoned theologians.

Many pastors and Bible teachers have brushed aside the preaching and teaching of end-time prophecy as too complex and controversial. Nevertheless, the closer we get to the fulfillment of end-time prophecies, the more interest people tend to show in knowing more about the Rapture and how and when it will occur.

Having studied both sides of the arguments, I can say, with every sense of humility, that pre-tribulation rapture doctrine is far more credible than any of the alternative doctrines especially the post-tribulation rapture doctrine because many biblical passages teach pre-tribulational rapture of the Church. The comparative merits of the pre-tribulation rapture views over post-tribulation rapture views are presented in the following discussions:

1. JESUS ALLUDED TO THE CONCEPT OF PRE-TRIBULATION RAPTURE

PRE-TRIB RAPTURE VIEW	POST-TRIB RAPTURE VIEW
The fact of the Rapture was first revealed by Christ to His disciples in John 14:1-3. This is the first New Testament intimation of the Rapture. Here Jesus promises to go and prepare a place for us and come again to take us to our mansions in His Father's house so where He is we may be also. These are plain statements that can only be interpreted literally. To do otherwise is to miss the mark. Interestingly, Paul expatiated on this in 1 **Thessalonians 4:13-18.** There is a strong tie between the Lord's revelation in **John 14:1-3** and Paul's exposition in **1 Thessalonians 4:13-18.** Christians who are alive will be re-united with those who have died in Christ before them and both groups will be taken to heaven as promised by Christ. This event, which is before the Tribulation is clearly different from His Second Coming, which occurs after the Tribulation. This translation is also echoed by Paul in **1 Corinthians 15:51-54.**	Proponents of post-tribulation rapture view have failed to acknowledge this fact. Concerning 1 Thessalonians 4:13-18, they argue that although Paul says that people will be snatched up to meet Christ in the air, he never says that Jesus turns around and goes back to heaven with the raptured saints for seven years.

COMMENTS

Posttribulational argument as stated above concerning 1 Thessalonians 4:13-18 is parochial because it fails to take cognizance of the fact that although none of the major passages about the Rapture explicitly mentions the return to heaven, John 14:1-3 specifically describes the return to heaven as the final venue of the rapture. Since the destination points to a venue in heaven, not on earth, the promise is consistent with a pre-tribulational rapture view and cannot point to a post-tribulational rapture.

2. CONSISTENT LITERAL INTERPRETATION

PRE-TRIB RAPTURE VIEW	POST-TRIB RAPTURE VIEW
Consistent literal interpretation is crucial to the proper understanding of what God is saying in the Bible. A golden rule of interpretation is that when the plain sense of Scripture makes sense, seek no further sense and take every word at its primary, ordinary, literal and usual meaning unless the facts of the context indicate clearly otherwise. Pretribulationalism is the only view that consistently follows a plain literal-grammatical interpretation of the prophetic portions of the Bible. The strict adherence to this principle has given credibility to its doctrine.	Posttribulationalism seems to ignore this principle in its general approach to eschatological interpretation. In their interpretation of John 14:3, they argue that Jesus is not promising to take believers to heaven and the reference to the many rooms in His Father's house should not be taken literally.

COMMENTS

Pretribulationalism is the only view that follows the normal literal-grammatical-historical interpretation of the Old and New Testament passages relating to the Rapture, the Great Tribulation and the Second Coming of Christ.

3. DISTINCTION BETWEEN ISRAEL AND THE CHURCH

PRE-TRIB RAPTURE VIEW	POST-TRIB RAPTURE VIEW
Dispensationalism teaches that God's prophetic programme has two distinct aspects – one for the Church and one for Israel. Only pretribulationism provides a purpose for the Rapture – which is to remove the Church so God can accomplish His programme with Israel during the seven-year Tribulation period. It is therefore imperative to distinguish passages God intended for Israel from those intended for the Church.	Generally, posttribulationists have not held to a clear distinction between the church and the nation of Israel in God's programme. Rather, they tend to include believers of all ages in the church by teaching replacement theology. The Church is considered to have replaced Israel in God's prophetic programme. Posttribulationism teaches this in order to justify its doctrine that the Church will go through the Tribulation.

COMMENTS

The expectation of the Church at the translation is to be taken into the Lord's presence, while the expectation of Israel at the Second Advent is to be taken into the Kingdom.

4. IMMINENCE

PRE-TRIB RAPTURE VIEW	POST-TRIB RAPTURE VIEW
When something is imminent, it means it could happen any moment. The New Testament speaks of our Lord's return as imminent, with passages instructing believers to watch, wait and get ready for the coming of the Lord, as no one knows when He will come. **Matthew 24:42;44** "Watch therefore, for you do not know what hour your Lord is coming" **Matthew 25:13** "Watch therefore, for you know neither the day nor the hour in which the Son of Man is coming" **Titus 2:13** "Looking for the blessed hope and glorious appearing of our great God and Savior Jesus Christ" Only pre-tribulationalism teaches imminent Rapture which requires neither specific signs leading to it nor time frame as a warning. Our primary duty as believers is to look, watch and wait for Christ's appearance and remain aware of His Second Coming and the signs that lead up to it.	Taking advantage of the fact that the word "imminent" is not mentioned in the Bible, proponents of postribulational rapture tend to deny the imminent nature of the Rapture. They fail to harmonise the various Scripture passages relating to the Rapture including **2 Peter 3:10-12.** The idea of imminence, according to the post-tribulation view, only applies to the wicked and the spiritually unprepared people that are still alive before the return of Christ.

COMMENTS
Although the word "imminent" is not used in Scripture, it has normally been considered to represent the view that the rapture could occur at any time. The danger of post-tribulation rapture view is its potential to encourage complacency among believers.

The hope offered the Church in the New Testament is the hope of rapture before the tribulation and not of survival through the tribulation.

5. MYSTERY

PRE-TRIB RAPTURE VIEW	POST-TRIB RAPTURE VIEW
In **1 Corinthians 15:51-54,** Paul speaks of the Rapture as a "mystery" which was later disclosed in **Col. 1:26 - "the mystery which has been hidden from ages and from generations, but now has been revealed to His saints."**	Posttribulationists have no credible alternative view to discredit the mystery element of the Rapture.
This is a once hidden truth of the past now revealed for the first time. Rapture is a separate event and a newly revealed mystery distinct from the Second Coming, which had been predicted in the Old Testament. Therefore, each of these events will happen at different times, that is, on either side of the seven-year Tribulation period.	

COMMENTS
1 Corinthians 2:7 declares:
" But we speak the wisdom of God in a mystery, the hidden wisdom which God ordained before the ages for our glory."
Ephesians 3:4-5
"By which, when you read, you may understand my knowledge in the mystery of Christ, which in other ages was not made known to the sons of men, as it has now been revealed by the Spirit to His holy apostles and prophets."

6. THE CHURCH IS NOT APPOINTED TO WRATH

PRE-TRIB RAPTURE VIEW	POST-TRIB RAPTURE VIEW
The fact that the word "Church" is not mentioned at all between Revelation 4 and 18 is convincing evidence that the Church will not be present on earth during the Tribulation. This is further buttressed by the following Bible passages that the Church will not experience the wrath of God. Revelation 3:10 "Because you have kept my command to persevere, I also will keep you from the hour of trial which shall come upon the whole world..." The possibility of a believer escaping the Tribulation is mentioned by Jesus: **Luke 24:36** **"Watch therefore, and pray always that you may be counted worthy to escape all these things that will come to pass and to stand before the Son of Man."** Other relevant passages are: **Romans 5:9** **1 Thessalonians 1:10** **1 Thessalonians 5:9**	**Posttributionists' main argument is that believers do not necessarily have to be removed from the world to be kept out of trouble. They point out that the Church will live during the Tribulation period but be kept from its wrath. The appearance of the word "saints" in Revelation Chapters 13, 16, 17 and 18 shows that the Church was in fact on the earth during the Tribulation. They further argue that the promise in Revelation 3:10 is a guarantee of being kept from the hour of Tribulation rather than from the trials of Tribulation suggesting that the hour means the "experience." In other words, the Church will live through the time but will not experience the events. They also point out that, historically, God's people have experienced times of intense persecution and trial. Therefore, they say, it should not be surprising that the church also experiences the Great Tribulation of the end times.**

COMMENTS

The word "saints" mentioned in those chapters of Revelation refers to the Tribulation saints and not the saints of the Church Age. Furthermore, if the events of the Tribulation are going to be global, affecting everybody, how can the Church be on earth and escape the experiences? The posttributionists' arguments are muddled, illogical and unclear. Their focus of the promise is on protection from the "hour", not from the "trial". However, God's promise In Revelation 3:10 is crystal clear – to keep the Church from the hour of trial which shall come upon he whole world. The pretribulational interpretation best preserves the promise of protection to the Church.

7. THE 70th WEEK OF DANIEL

PRE-TRIB RAPTURE VIEW	POST-TRIB RAPTURE VIEW
The 70th Week of Daniel represents a week of years equating 7 years. This period corresponds to the Tribulation period during which God's prophetic programme concerning Israel will be accomplished. This is amplified in the following passages: **Daniel 12:1** ".....And there shall be a time of trouble such as never has been since there was a nation till that time. But at that time your people shall be delivered, everyone whose name shall be found written in the book." **Jeremiah 30:7** "Alas! That day is so great there is none like it; it is a time of distress for Jacob; yet he shall be saved out of it."	Posttribulationists argue that as far as God's prophetic programme is concerned, the Church has replaced Israel and the 144,000 Jews and the great multitude of Revelation 7 are included in the Church and that all living believers will be raptured at the end of the Tribulation.

COMMENTS

Post-tribulationism fails to recognise God's prophetic programme for the Church as distinct from His programme for Israel. This has led to the wrong conclusion that the Church is going to experience the wrath of God in the Tribulation.

At the beginning of the 70th week, which is the Tribulation Period, the Antichrist will enter into a covenant with Israel offering her political protection. However, at the mid-point of the seven-year Tribulation Period, the Antichrist will break the covenant. This will mark the beginning of the Great Tribulation of which Christ spoke in Matthew 24:15-26.

The Church will be raptured before the beginning of the 70th Week of Daniel which described as the Day of the Lord, otherwise known as the Tribulation period.

8. THE NECESSITY OF AN INTERVAL BETWEEN THE RAPTURE AND THE SECOND COMING

PRE-TRIB RAPTURE VIEW	POST-TRIB RAPTURE VIEW
The Tribulation period creates a time interval between the Rapture (when Jesus comes for His bride) and the Second Coming when He comes with His Bride to the earth. For the marriage of the Lamb and the marriage supper to take place in heaven (**Revelation 19:7-9**), there must, of necessity, be a time interval between the Rapture and the Second Coming of Christ. The announcement about the marriage and the marriage supper was made in heaven before the Second Coming of Christ. In other words, the coming of Christ for His bride (Rapture) must take place before the marriage, the marriage feast and finally the Second Coming to the earth. The marriage and the feast cannot take place in the air while the Church (the Bride) is on the earth. **Separation of the sheep from the goat (Matthew 25:32)** If the Rapture took place at the same time as the Second Coming of Christ, there would be no need of separating the sheep from the goat, as the separation would have taken place at the Rapture. Clearly, the separation will be necessitated by the time interval between the Rapture and the Second Coming According to **2 Corinthians 5:10**, all believers of Church Age must appear before the judgment seat of Christ in heaven after the Rapture, but this event is never mentioned in the detailed account connected with the Second Coming of Christ	Post-tribulation rapture theory teaches that both the Rapture and the Second Coming will happen simultaneously. Believers will be raptured and then immediately make a U-turn and come back to earth with Christ.

COMMENTS
A time interval is necessary for a proper harmonisation of Scriptures. Firstly, there could be no marriage if the Groom was in heaven while the bride remained on earth.
If the translation through the Rapture had taken place simultaneously with the Second Coming, there would be no need of separating the sheep from the goats at the subsequent judgment as the separation would have taken place in the very act of the translation.

9. CONTRASTS BETWEEN THE RAPURE AND THE SECOND COMING

PRE-TRIB RAPTURE VIEW	POST-TRIB RAPTURE VIEW
1. The Rapture is described as imminent, with no hint of signs, while The Second Coming is preceded by a series of defined signs. 2. The Rapture of the Church is pictured before the Tribulation while the Second Coming is followed by the deliverance of the Tribulation saints. 3. At the Rapture the sinful world is not judged but at the Second Coming the world will be judged 4. At the Rapture the Church saints meet Christ in the air while at the Second Coming Christ returns to meet the Tribulation saints on earth. 5. At the Rapture the Mount of Olives remain unchanged while at the Second Coming the Mount of Olive will split in two – Zechariah 14:4-5. 6. At the Rapture, the Lord Himself comes down to meet the Church and living saints are translated but at the Second Coming, the angels gather the elect and believers are not translated. 7. Satan is not bound at the Rapture but he is bound at the Second Coming.	Posttribulationists believe that the Rapture and the Second Coming will happen simultaneously. They argue that the gathering of the elect in Matthew 24:31 is a reference to the rapture, making no distinction between the timing of the Rapture and the Second Coming, They strongly believe that the Bible simply does not teach a two-phase Second Coming.

COMMENTS

Posttribulationists err in interpreting theRapture and the Second Coming by failing to make a clear distinction between them and therleading many to mi

Furthermore, the separation of the sheep and goats at His Second Coming would be redundant if the sheep had already been separated at the Rapture.

10. THE WORK OF THE HOLY SPIRIT

PRE-TRIB RAPTURE VIEW	POST - TRIB RAPTURE VIEW
The Holy Spirit (The Restrainer) must be taken out of the world before the lawless one (The Antichrist, who dominates the Tribulation Period) can be revealed. In other words, the Church, which the Holy Spirit indwells, must be raptured before the emergence of the antichrist during the Tribulation period. In essence, the Rapture must take place before the beginning of the Tribulation Period. 2 Thessalonians 2:6-8 "And now you know what is restraining, that he may be revealed in his own time. For the mystery of lawlessness is already at work; Only He who now restrains will do so until He is taken out of the way. And then the lawless one will be revealed, whom the Lord will consume with the breath of His mouth and destroy with the brightness of His Coming."	The post-tribulation rapture view argues that since Paul did not specifically mention the Holy Spirit in this passage, it is difficult to accept the Holy Spirit as the identity of the Restrainer. Even if the Holy Spirit is the Restrainer, all Paul seems to be saying in this passage is that He is ceasing His work of restraining evil, not that He is necessarily gone from the earth.

COMMENTS

Paul did not have to specifically identify who the restrainer is since the Thessalonians already knew by deduction from the previous passages. Paul had assured them that they were not yet living in the Day of the Lord, that is, the end-time divine judgment had not yet begun.

There is overwhelming evidence to believe that the Restrainer is none other than the Holy Spirit working through the New Testament Church.

A GREAT PROMISE FROM OUR LORD JESUS CHRIST

One of the greatest promises in the Bible is that made by Jesus in John 14:1-3 that He will come back again and take us to heaven so that wherever He is there we will be also. This promise, which was not made lightly as it came from the Lord Himself, is clearly a reference to the Rapture phase of His coming, which is distinct from His Second Coming to earth as recorded in Acts 1:11, Matthew 24:29-30 and Revelation 19:11-14. Since Jesus did fulfil all prophecies about His first coming, we can know with absolute certainty that He will come back one day to rapture His Church to be with Him in heaven. The pre-tribulation rapture view is the only theory that corroborates the Lord's promise in its entirety. He has gone ahead of us to prepare a place for us, and He is coming back to take us to heaven to occupy the incredible mansions. The natural question is: When? The simple answer is: Any moment.

From the above, it is evident that the Rapture is not the same event as the Second Coming of Christ, and both cannot possibly occur simultaneously. The rapture is imminent and could take place at any time but not so with the Second Coming, which will be preceded by specific signs and the seven-year Tribulation Period. Even though no single Bible passage indicates precisely when the Rapture will take place in relation to the Tribulation in a way that would settle the issue to everyone's satisfaction, it does not mean that the Bible does not teach a clear position on the subject matter. In-depth and unbiased studies of end-time prophecies over the time have produced conclusive evidence that the Rapture and the Second Coming cannot possibly occur simultaneously. This rational conclusion could only be achieved through the harmonisation of different Bible passages and application of consistent literal interpretation. This exactly is the approach adopted by pre-tribulation rapture viewpoint.

Now is the time to lay aside every argument that is capable of getting us distracted from "looking for the blessed hope and glorious appearing of our great God and Saviour Jesus Christ" – Titus 2:13. As the world

THE RAPTURE AND THE SECOND COMING EXPLAINED

is passing away with its desires, we should be waiting and watching in expectation of the Rapture occurring any moment lest we are caught unawares. Our Lord enjoins us several times to "watch" and "be ready". How can we ignore such a great warning!

Adopting a pre-tribulation rapture view encourages us to live right in constant state of readiness to be raptured.

I pray we shall not be left behind.

DIAGRAM OF THE SEVEN SEALS, SEVEN TRUMPETS AND SEVEN BOWLS

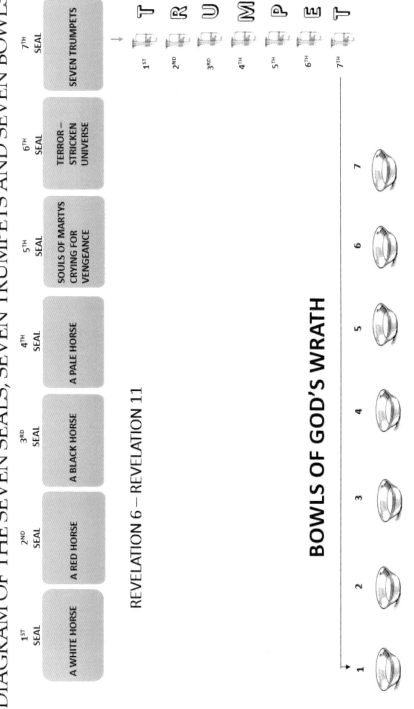

1ST SEAL	2ND SEAL	3RD SEAL	4TH SEAL	5TH SEAL	6TH SEAL	7TH SEAL
A WHITE HORSE	A RED HORSE	A BLACK HORSE	A PALE HORSE	SOULS OF MARTYS CRYING FOR VENGEANCE	TERROR – STRICKEN UNIVERSE	SEVEN TRUMPETS

REVELATION 6 – REVELATION 11

T R U M P E T

1ST 2ND 3RD 4TH 5TH 6TH 7TH

BOWLS OF GOD'S WRATH

1 2 3 4 5 6 7